glencoe

teenhealth

conflict resolution
+ violence prevention

McGraw Hill Education

Bothell, WA • Chicago, IL • Columbus, OH • New York, NY

Meet the Authors

Mary H. Bronson, Ph.D. recently retired after teaching for 30 years in Texas public schools. Dr. Bronson taught health education in grades K–12 as well as health education methods classes at the graduate and undergraduate levels. As Health Education Specialist for the Dallas School District, Dr. Bronson developed and implemented a district-wide health eduation program. She has been honored as Texas Health Educator of the Year by the Texas Association for Health, Physical Education, Recreation, and Dance and selected Teacher of the Year twice by her colleagues. Dr. Bronson has assisted school districts throughout the country in developing local health education programs. She is also the coauthor of Glencoe Health.

Michael J. Cleary, Ed.D., C.H.E.S. is a professor at Slippery Rock University, where he teaches methods courses and supervises field experiences. Dr. Cleary taught health education at Evanston Township High School in Illinois and later served as the Lead Teacher Specialist at the McMillen Center for Health Education in Fort Wayne, Indiana. Dr. Cleary has published widely on curriculum development and assessment in K–12 and college health education. Dr. Cleary is also coauthor of Glencoe Health.

Betty M. Hubbard, Ed.D., C.H.E.S. has taught science and health education in grades 6–12 as well as undergraduate- and graduate-level courses. She is a professor at the University of Central Arkansas, where in addition to teaching she conducts in-service training for health education teachers in school districts throughout Arkansas. In 1991, Dr. Hubbard received the university's teaching excellence award. Her publications, grants, and presentations focus on research-based, comprehensive health instruction. Dr. Hubbard is a fellow of the American Association for Health Education and serves as the contributing editor of the Teaching Ideas feature of the American Journal of Health Education.

Contributing Author

Dinah Zike, M.Ed. is an international curriculum consultant and inventor who has designed and developed educational products and three-dimensional, interactive graphic organizers for more than 35 years. As president and founder of Dinah-Might Adventures, L.P., Dinah is author of more than 100 award-winning educational publications. Dinah has a B.S. and an M.S. in educational curriculum and instruction from Texas A&M University. Dinah Zike's Foldables® are an exclusive feature of McGraw-Hill.

MHEonline.com

Send all inquiries to:
McGraw-Hill Education
STEM Learning Solutions Center
8787 Orion Place
Columbus, OH 43240

ISBN: 978-0-07-664045-4
MHID: 0-07-664045-0

Printed in the United States of America.

6 7 8 9 LMN 20 19

STEM McGraw-Hill is committed to providing instructional materials in Science, Technology, Engineering, and Mathematics (STEM) that give all students a solid foundation, one that prepares them for college and careers in the 21st century.

Reviewers

Professional Reviewers

Amy Eyler, Ph.D., CHES
Washington University in St. Louis
St. Louis, Missouri

Shonali Saha, M.D.
Johns Hopkins School of Medicine
Baltimore, Maryland

Roberta Duyff
Duyff & Associates
St. Louis, MO

Teacher Reviewers

Lou Ann Donlan
Altoona Area School District
Altoona, PA

Steve Federman
Loveland Intermediate School
Loveland, Ohio

Rick R. Gough
Ashland Middle School
Ashland, Ohio

Jacob Graham
Oblock Junior High
Plum, Pennsylvania

William T. Gunther
Clarkston Community Schools
Clarkston, MI

Ellie Hancock
Somerset Area School District
Somerset, PA

Diane Hursky
Independence Middle School
Bethel Park, PA

Veronique Javier
Thomas Cardoza Middle School
Jackson, Mississippi

Patricia A. Landon
Patrick F. Healy Middle School
East Orange, NJ

Elizabeth Potash
Council Rock High School South
Holland, PA

The Path to Good Health

Your health book has many features that will aid you in your learning. Some of these features are listed below. You can use the map at the right to help you find these and other special features in the book.

* The **Big Idea** can be found at the start of each lesson.

* Your **Foldables**® help you organize your notes.

* The **Quick Write** at the start of each lesson will help you think about the topic and give you an opportunity to write about it in your journal.

* The **Bilingual Glossary** contains vocabulary terms and definitions in Spanish and English.

* **Health Skills Activities** help you learn more about each of the 10 health skills.

* **Infographs** provide a colorful, visual way to learn about current health news and trends.

* The **Fitness Zone** provides an online fitness resource that includes podcasts, videos, activity cards, and more!

* **Hands-On Health Activities** give you the opportunity to complete hands-on projects.

* **Videos** encourage you to explore real life health topics.

* **Audio** directs you to online audio chapter summaries.

* **Web Quest** activities challenge you to relate lesson concepts to current health news and research.

* **Review** your understanding of health concepts with lesson reviews and quizzes.

What's the word on the street? The **glossary** lists vocabulary terms in English and Spanish.

Quick! Write about your good health habits using a **Quick Write** activity.

Think big! Start your journey with a **Big Idea** and increase your pace with **Foldables**®.

iv

Sharpen your skills with **Health Skills Activities**.

Got a nose for news? Check out each chapter's **infographs** for health news and trends.

Get into the zone –the **Fitness Zone!** Listen to podcasts, watch videos, and more.

Show what you know by completing a **Hands-On Health Activity**.

Stop! Look and Listen! Watch a Health eSpotlight **video** and explore real life health topics. Listen to the **audio** summaries to review the chapter.

Go on a quest. Take a **Web Quest** to learn more about health news and research.

Finish strong! **Review** your understanding of health concepts with lesson reviews and quizzes.

Contents

F4F-1 through F4F-9
Flip your book over to see a special section on fitness.

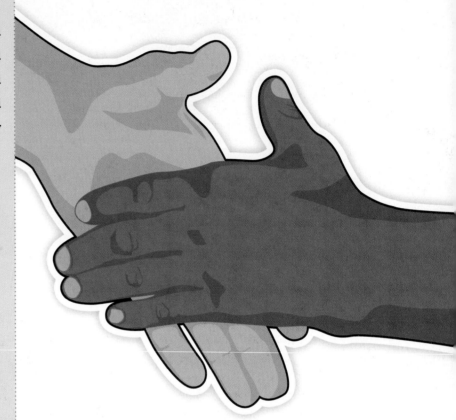

chapter

1 Conflict Resolution

Your Total Health

WHAT IS HEALTH?

Do you know someone you would describe as "healthy"? What kinds of traits do they have? Maybe they are involved in sports. Maybe they just "look" healthy. Looking fit and feeling well are important, but there is more to having good health. Good health also includes getting along well with others and feeling good about yourself.

Your **physical**, **emotional**, and **social** *health* are all **related** and make up your *total* **health.**

Health, the *combination of physical, mental/emotional, and social well-being,* may look like the sides of a triangle. You need all three sides to make the triangle. Each side supports the other two sides. Your physical health, mental/emotional health, and social health are all related and make up your total health.

Physical Health

Physical health is one side of the health triangle. Engaging in physical activity every day will help to build and maintain your physical health. Some of the ways you can improve your physical health include the following:

* **EATING HEALTHY FOODS** Choose nutritious meals and snacks.

* **VISITING THE DOCTOR REGULARLY** Get regular checkups from a doctor and a dentist.

* **CARING FOR PERSONAL HYGIENE** Shower or bathe each day. Brush and floss your teeth at least twice every day.

* **WEARING PROTECTIVE GEAR** When playing sports, using protective gear and following safety rules will help you avoid injuries.

* **GET ENOUGH SLEEP** Most teens need about nine hours of sleep every night.

You can also have good physical health by avoiding harmful behaviors, such as using alcohol, tobacco, and other drugs. The use of tobacco has been linked to many diseases, such as heart disease and cancer.

Mental/Emotional Health

Another side of the health triangle is your mental/emotional health. How do you handle your feelings, thoughts, and emotions each day? You can improve your mental/emotional health by talking and thinking about yourself in a healthful way. Share your thoughts and feelings with your family, a trusted adult, or with a friend.

If you are mentally and emotionally healthy, you can face challenges in a positive way. Be patient with yourself when you try to learn new subjects or new skills. Remember that everybody makes mistakes—including you! Next time you can do better.

Taking action to reach your goals is another way to develop good mental/emotional health. This can help you focus your energy and give you a sense of accomplishment. Make healthful choices, keep your promises, and take responsibility for what you do, and you will feel good about yourself and your life.

Social Health

A third side of the health triangle is your social health. Social health means how you relate to people at home, at school, and everywhere in your world. Strong friendships and family relationships are signs of good social health.

Do you get along well with your friends, classmates, and teachers? Do you spend time with your family? You can develop skills for having good relationships. Good social health includes supporting the people you care about. It also includes communicating with, respecting, and valuing people. Sometimes you may disagree with others. You can disagree and express your thoughts, but be thoughtful and choose your words carefully.

Your total health is made up of three parts, like a triangle.

MENTAL/EMOTIONAL HEALTH

YOUR TOTAL HEALTH is a combination of physical, mental/emotional, and social health.

PHYSICAL HEALTH

SOCIAL HEALTH

ACHIEVING WELLNESS

What is the difference between health and wellness? Wellness is *a state of well-being or balanced health over a long period of time.* Your health changes from day to day. One day you may feel tired if you did not get enough sleep. Maybe you worked very hard at sports

practice. The next day, you might feel well rested and full of energy because you rested. Your emotions also change. You might feel sad one day but happy the next day.

Your overall health is like a snapshot of your physical, mental/emotional, and social health. Your wellness takes

a longer view. Being healthy means balancing the three sides of your health triangle over weeks or months. Wellness is sometimes represented by a continuum, or scale, that gives a picture of your health at a certain time. It may also tell you how well you are taking care of yourself.

The Mind-Body Connection

Your emotions have a lot to do with your physical health. Think about an event in your own life that made you feel sad. How did you deal with this emotion? Sometimes people have a difficult time dealing with their emotions. This can have a negative effect on their physical health. For example, they might get headaches, backaches, upset stomachs, colds, the flu, or even more serious diseases. Why do you think this happens?

Your mind and body connect through your nervous system. This system includes thousands of miles of nerves. The nerves link your brain to your body. Upsetting thoughts and feelings sometimes affect the signals from your brain to other parts of your body.

Your **emotions** have *a lot* to do with *your* **physical health.**

The mind-body connection describes *how your emotions affect your physical and overall health and how your overall health affects your emotions.* This connection shows again how important it is to keep the three sides of the health triangle balanced. If you become very sad or angry, or if you have other strong emotions, talk to someone. Sometimes talking to a good friend helps. Sometimes you may need the services of a counselor or a medical professional.

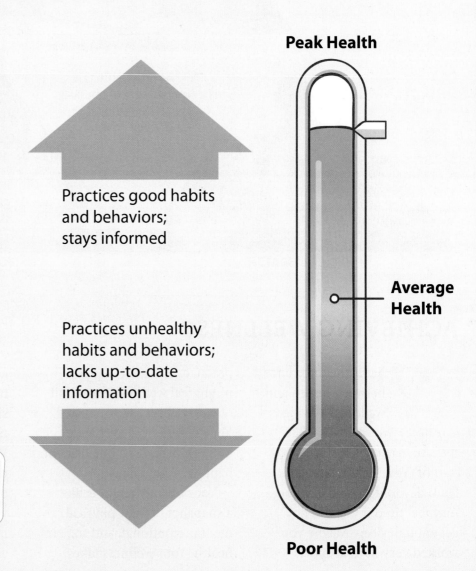

Practices good habits and behaviors; stays informed

Practices unhealthy habits and behaviors; lacks up-to-date information

Peak Health

Average Health

Poor Health

The Wellness Scale identifies how healthy you are at a given point in time.

x

Health Influences *and* Risk Factors

WHAT INFLUENCES YOUR HEALTH?

What are your favorite foods or activities? Your answers reflect your personal tastes, or likes and dislikes. Your health is influenced by your personal tastes and by many other factors such as:

- heredity
- environment
- family and friends
- culture
- media
- attitudes
- behavior

Heredity

You can control some of these factors, but not all of them. For example, you cannot control the natural color of your hair or eyes. Heredity (huh•RED•i•tee) is *the passing of traits from parents to their biological children.* Heredity determines the color of your eyes and hair, and other physical traits, or parts of your appearance. Genes are the basic units of heredity. They are made from chemicals called DNA, and they create the pattern for your physical traits. You inherited, or received, half of your DNA from your mother and half from your father.

Environment

Think about where you live. Do you live in a city, a suburb, a small town, or in a rural area? Where you live is the physical part of your environment (en•VY•ruhn•mehnt), or *all the living and nonliving things around you.*

Environment is another factor that affects your personal health. Your physical environment includes the home you live in, the school you attend, and the air and water around you.

Your *social environment* includes the people in your life. They can be friends, classmates, and neighbors. Your friends and peers, or *people close to you in age who are a lot like you,* may influence your choices.

You may feel pressure to think and act like them. Peer pressure can also influence health choices. The influence can be positive or negative. Helping a friend with homework, volunteering with a friend, or simply listening to a friend are examples of positive peer influence. A friend who wants you to drink alcohol, for example, is a negative influence. Recreation is also a part of your social environment. Playing games and enjoying physical activities with others can have a positive effect on your health.

Traits such as eye and hair color are inherited from parents.

Culture

Your family is one of the biggest influences on your life. It shapes your **cultural background,** or *the beliefs, customs, and traditions of a specific group of people.* You learned that your family influences your health. In addition to your family, your **culture,** or *the collected beliefs, customs, and behaviors of a group,* also affects your health. Your family and their culture may influence the foods you eat as well as the activities and special events you celebrate with special foods. Some families fast (do not eat food) during religious events. Ahmed's family observes the holiday of Ramadan.

During this holiday, members of his family fast until sundown. Your family might also celebrate traditions that include dances, foods, ceremonies, songs, and games. Your culture can also affect your health. Knowing how your lifestyle and family history relate to health problems can help you stay well.

Media

What do television, radio, movies, magazines, newspapers, books, billboards, and the Internet have in common? They are all forms of **media,** or *various methods for communicating information.* The media is another factor that affects your personal health.

The media provide powerful sources of information and influence.

You may learn helpful new facts about health on the Internet or television. You might also see a commercial for the latest video game or athletic shoes. The goal of commercials on television or the Internet, as well as advertisements in print, is to make you want to buy a product. The product may be good or bad for your health. You can make wise health choices by learning to **evaluate,** or *determine the quality* of everything you see, hear, or read.

The celebration of Kwanzaa is a tradition in many African American families.

YOUR BEHAVIOR AND YOUR HEALTH

Do you protect your skin from the sun? Do you get enough sleep so that you are not tired during the day? Do you eat healthful foods? Do you listen to a friend who needs to talk about a problem? Your answers to these questions reflect your personal lifestyle factors, or *the behaviors and habits that help determine a person's level of health.* Positive lifestyle factors promote good health. Negative lifestyle factors promote poor health.

Positive lifestyle factors promote **good** health.

Your attitude, or your *feelings and beliefs,* toward your personal lifestyle factors plays an important role in your health. You will also have greater success in managing your health if you keep a positive attitude. Teens who have a positive attitude about their health are more likely to practice good health habits and take responsibility for their health.

Risk Behaviors

"Dangerous intersection. Proceed with caution." "Don't walk." "No lifeguard on duty." You have probably seen these signs or similar signs. They are posted to warn you about possible risks or dangers and to keep you safe.

 Eating well-balanced meals, starting with a good breakfast.

 Getting at least 60 minutes of physical activity daily.

 Sleeping at least eight hours every night.

 Doing your best in school and other activities.

 Avoiding tobacco, alcohol, and other drugs.

 Following safety rules and wearing protective gear.

 Relating well to family, friends, and classmates.

Lifestyle factors affect your personal health.

Risk, or *the chance that something harmful may happen to your health and wellness,* is part of everyday life. Some risks are easy to identify. Everyday tasks such as preparing food with a knife or crossing a busy street both carry some risk. Other risks are more hidden. Some foods you like might be high in fat.

You cannot avoid every kind of risk. However, the risks you can avoid often involve risk behavior. A risk behavior is an action or behavior that might cause injury or harm to you or others. Playing a sport can be risky, but if you wear protective gear, you may avoid injury. Wear a helmet when you ride a bike to avoid the risk of a head injury if you fall. Smoking cigarettes is another risk behavior that you can avoid. Riding in a car without a safety belt is a risk behavior you can avoid by buckling up. Another risk behavior is having a lifestyle with little physical activity, such as sitting in front of the TV or a computer instead of being active. You can avoid many kinds of risk by taking responsibility for your personal health behaviors and avoiding risk.

RISKS AND CONSEQUENCES
All risk behaviors have consequences. Some consequences are minor or short-term. You might eat a sweet snack just before dinner so that you lose your appetite for a healthy meal. Other risk behaviors may have serious or life-threatening consequences. These are long-term consequences.

Experimenting with alcohol, tobacco, or other drugs has long-term consequences that can seriously damage your health. They can affect all three sides of your health triangle. They can lead to dangerous addictions, which are physical and mental dependencies.

These substances can confuse the user's judgment and can increase the risks he or she takes. Using these substances may also lead to problems with family and friends, and problems at school.

Risks that affect your health are more complicated when they are cumulative risks (KYOO•myuh•luh•tiv), which occur *when one risk factor adds to another to increase danger.* For example, making unhealthy food choices is one risk. Not getting regular physical activity is another risk. Add these two risks together over time, and you raise your risk of developing diseases such as heart disease and cancer.

Many choices you make affect your health. Knowing the consequences of your choices and behaviors can help you take responsibility for your health.

Reducing Risks

Practicing prevention, *taking steps to avoid something,* is the best way to deal with risks. For example, wear a helmet when you ride a bike to help prevent head injury. Slow down when walking or running on wet or icy pavement to help prevent a fall. Prevention also means watching out for possible dangers. When you know dangers are ahead, you can avoid them and prevent accidents.

Physical injury can be a consequence of risk behaviors.

STAYING INFORMED You can take responsibility for your health by staying informed. Learn about developments in health to maintain your own health. Getting a physical exam at least once a year by a doctor is another way to stay informed about your health.

CHOOSING ABSTINENCE
If you practice abstinence from risk behaviors, you care for your own health and others' health by preventing illness and injury. Abstinence is *the conscious, active choice not to participate in high-risk behaviors.* By choosing not to use tobacco, you may avoid getting lung cancer. By staying away from alcohol, illegal drugs, and sexual activity, you avoid the negative consequences of these risk behaviors.

Abstinence is good for all sides of your health triangle. It promotes your physical health by helping you avoid injury and illness. It protects your mental/emotional health by giving you peace of mind. It also benefits your relationships with family members, peers, and friends. Practicing abstinence shows you are taking responsibility for your personal health behaviors and that you respect yourself and others. You can feel good about making positive health choices, which will strengthen your mental/emotional health as well as your social health.

☑ Plan ahead.

☑ Think about consequences.

☑ Resist negative pressure from others.

☑ Stay away from risk takers.

☑ Pay attention to what you are doing.

☑ Know your limits.

☑ Be aware of dangers.

Reducing risk behaviors will help maintain your overall health.

Getting regular checkups is one form of prevention.

Building Health Skills

SKILLS FOR A HEALTHY LIFE

Health skills are *skills that help you become and stay healthy.* Health skills can help you improve your physical, mental/emotional, and social health. Just as you learn math, reading, sports, and other kinds of skills, you can learn skills for taking care of your health now and for your entire life.

These ten skills affect your physical, mental/emotional, and social health and can benefit you throughout your life.

Health Skills	What It Means to You
Accessing Information	You know how to find valid and reliable health information and health-promoting products and services.
Practicing Healthful Behaviors	You take action to reduce risks and protect yourself against illness and injury.
Stress Management	You find healthy ways to reduce and manage stress in your life.
Analyzing Influences	You recognize the many factors that influence your health, including culture, media, and technology.
Communication Skills	You express your ideas and feelings and listen when others express theirs.
Refusal Skills	You can say no to risky behaviors.
Conflict-Resolution Skills	You can work out problems with others in healthful ways.
Decision Making	You think through problems and find healthy solutions.
Goal Setting	You plan for the future and work to make your plans come true.
Advocacy	You take a stand for the common good and make a difference in your home, school, and community.

SELF-MANAGEMENT SKILLS

When you were younger, your parents and other adults decided what was best for your health. Now that you are older, you make many of these decisions for yourself. You take care of your personal health. You are developing your self-management skills. Two key self-management skills are practicing healthful behaviors and managing stress. When you eat healthy foods and get enough sleep, you are taking actions that promote good health. Stress management is learning to cope with challenges that put a strain on you mentally or emotionally.

Practicing Healthful Behaviors

Your behaviors affect your physical, mental/emotional, and social health. You will see benefits quickly when you practice healthful behaviors. If you exercise regularly, your heart and muscles grow stronger. When you eat healthful foods and drink plenty of water, your body works well.

Getting a good night's sleep will help you wake up with more energy. Respecting and caring for others will help you develop healthy relationships. Managing your feelings in positive ways will help you avoid actions you may regret later.

Staying **positive** is a **good health** *habit.*

Practicing healthful behaviors can help prevent injury, illness, and other health problems. When you practice healthful actions, you can help your total health. Your total health means your physical, mental/emotional, and social health. This means you take care of yourself and do not take risks. It means you learn health-promoting habits. When you eat well-balanced meals and

healthful snacks and get regular physical checkups you are practicing good health habits. Staying positive is another good health habit.

Managing Stress

Learning ways to deal with **stress,** *the body's response to real or imagined dangers or other life events,* is an important self-management skill. Stress management can help you learn ways to deal with stress. Stress management means identifying sources of stress. It also means you learn how to handle stress in ways that support good health. Relaxation is a good way to deal with stress. Exercise is another way to positively deal with stress.

Studying for a test can cause stress.

Making Decisions and Setting Goals

The path to good health begins with making good decisions. You may make more of your own decisions now. Some of those decisions might be deciding which clothes to buy or which classes to take.

As you grow older, you gain more freedom, but with it comes more responsibility. You will need to understand the short-term and long-term consequences of decisions.

Another responsibility is goal setting. You also need to plan how to reach those goals.

When you learn how to set realistic goals, you take a step toward health and well-being. Learning to make decisions and to set goals will help give you purpose and direction in your life.

ACCESSING INFORMATION

Knowing how to get reliable, or *trust-worthy and dependable,* health information is an important skill. Where can you find all this information? A main source is from adults you can trust. Community resources give you other ways to get information. These include the library and government health agencies. Organizations such as the American Red Cross can also provide good information.

Getting health information is important, but so is analyzing whether that health information is valid, or reliable. Carefully review web sites ending in .org.

Many of these sites are maintained by organizations, such as the American Cancer Society or American Diabetes Association. However, some sites ending in .org may not be legitimate.

Reliable Sources

You can find facts about health and health-enhancing products or services through media sources such as television, radio, and the Internet. TV and radio interviews with health professionals can give you information about current scientific studies related to health.

Web sites that end in .gov and .edu are often the most reliable sites. These sites are maintained by government organizations and educational institutions.

The Internet can be a good source of health information.

xviii

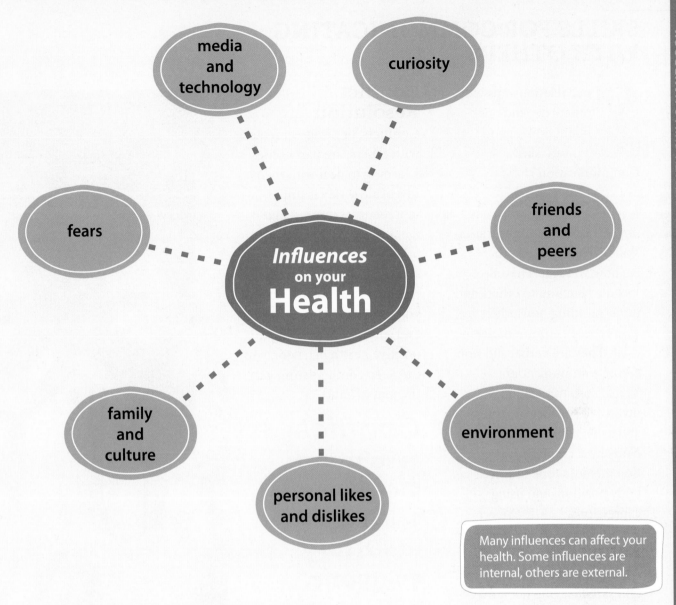

media and technology

curiosity

fears

friends and peers

Influences on your **Health**

family and culture

personal likes and dislikes

environment

Many influences can affect your health. Some influences are internal, others are external.

Analyzing Influences

Learning how to analyze health information, products, and services will help you act in ways that protect your health. The first step in analyzing an influence is to identify its source. A TV commercial may tell you a certain food has health benefits.

Your **decisions** have to do with your *own* **values** and **beliefs.**

Ask yourself who is the source of the information. Next, think about the motive, or reason, for the influence. Does the advertiser really take your well-being into consideration? Does the ad make you curious about the product?

Does it try to scare you into buying the product? Analyzing influences involves recognizing factors that affect or influence your health.

Your decisions also have to do with your own values and beliefs. The opinions of your friends and family members affect your decisions. Your culture and messages from the media also affect your decisions.

xix

SKILLS FOR COMMUNICATING WITH OTHERS

Your relationships with others depend on maintaining good **communication** skills. Communication is *the exchange of information through the use of words or actions.* Good communication skills include telling others how you feel. They also include listening to others and understanding how others feel. Two types of communication exist. They are verbal and nonverbal communication. Verbal communication involves a speaker or writer, and a listener or reader. Nonverbal communication includes tone of voice, body position, and using expressions.

Refusal Skills

An important communication skill is saying no. It may be something that is wrong. It may be something that you are not comfortable doing. You may worry what will happen if you don't go along with the group. Will your friends still like you? Will you still be a part of the group? It is at these times that **refusal skills,** or *strategies that help you say no effectively,* can help. Using refusal skills can sometimes be challenging, but they can help you stay true to yourself and to your beliefs. Also, other people will have respect for you for being honest.

Conflict Resolution

Conflicts, or disagreements with others, are part of life. Learning to deal with them in a healthy way is important. **Conflict resolution** is *a life skill that involves solving a disagreement in a way that satisfies both sides.* Conflict-resolution skills can help you find a way to satisfy everyone. Also, by using this positive health behavior, you can keep conflicts from getting out of hand.

Conflict **resolution** skills can help you find a way to *satisfy* **everyone.**

Advocacy

People with **advocacy** skills *take action in support of a cause.* They work to bring about a change by speaking out for something like health and wellness. When you speak out for health, you encourage other people to live healthy lives. Advocacy also means keeping others informed.

Using refusal skills effectively can help you avoid potentially dangerous situation.

Making Decisions *and* Setting Goals

DECISIONS AND YOUR HEALTH

As you grow up, you usually gain more privileges. Along with privileges comes responsibility. You will make more of your own decisions. The choices and decisions you make can affect each part of your health triangle.

As you get older, you will learn to make more important decisions. You will need to understand the short-term and long-term consequences of the decisions you make.

You can learn the skill of making good decisions.

Some decisions may help you avoid harmful behaviors. These questions can help you understand some of the consequences of health-related decisions.

- How will this decision affect my health?
- Will it affect the health of others? If so, how?
- Is the behavior I might choose harmful or illegal?
- How will my family feel about my decision?
- Does this decision fit with my values?
- How will this decision affect my goals?

THE DECISION-MAKING PROCESS

You make decisions every day. Some decisions are easy to make. Other decisions are more difficult. Understanding the process of decision making, or *the process of making a choice or solving a problem,* will help you make the best possible decisions. The decision-making process can be broken down into six steps. You can apply these six steps to any decision you need to make.

Step 1: State the Situation

Identify the situation as you understand it. When you understand the situation and your choices you can make a sound decision. Ask yourself: What choice do you need to make? What are the facts? Who else is involved?

Step 2: List the Options

When you feel like you understand your situation, think of your options. List all of the possibilities you can think of. Be sure to include only those options that are safe. It is also important to ask an adult you trust for advice when making an important decision.

Step 3: Weigh the Possible Outcomes

After listing your options, you need to evaluate the consequences of each option. The word H.E.L.P. can be used to work through this step of the decision-making process.

- **H** (Healthful) What health risks will this option present to me and to others?
- **E** (Ethical) Does this choice reflect what my family and I believe to be ethical, or right? Does this choice show respect for me and others?
- **L** (Legal) Will I be breaking the law? Is this legal for someone my age?
- **P** (Parent Approval) Would my parents approve of this choice?

Step 4: Consider Your Values

Always consider your values or the beliefs that guide the way you live. Your values reflect what is important to you and what you have learned is right and wrong. Honesty, respect, consideration, and good health are values.

Step 5: Make a Decision and Act

You've weighed your options. You've considered the risks and consequences. Now you're ready for action. Choose the option that seems best for you. Remember that this step is not complete until you take action.

Step 6: Evaluate the Decision

Evaluating the results can help you make better decisions in the future. To evaluate the results, ask yourself: Was the outcome positive or negative? Were there any unexpected outcomes? Was there anything you could have done differently? How did your decision affect others? Do you think you made the right decision? What have you learned from the experience? If the outcome was not what you expected, try again.

Understanding the decision-making process will help you make sound decisions.

Step 1 State the situation.

Step 2 List the options.

Step 3 Weigh the possible outcomes.

Step 4 Consider your values.

Step 5 Make a decision and act.

Step 6 Evaluate the decision.

SETTING REALISTIC GOALS

When you think about your future, what do you see? Do you see someone who has graduated from college and has a good job? Are there things you want to achieve? Answering these questions can give you an idea of your goals in life. A goal is something you want to accomplish.

Goal setting is *the process of working toward something you want to accomplish.* When you have learned to set realistic goals, they can help you focus on what you want to accomplish in life. Realistic goals are goals you can reach.

Setting goals can benefit your health. Many goals can help to improve your overall health. Think about all you want to accomplish in life. Do you need to set some health-related goals to be able to accomplish those things?

Goals can become milestones and can tell you how far you have come. Reaching goals can be a powerful boost to your self-confidence. Improving your self-confidence can help to strengthen your mental/emotional health.

Types of Goals

There are two basic types of goals—short-term goals, *goals that you can achieve in a short length of time,* and long-term goals, *goals that you plan to reach over an extended period of time.* As the names imply, short-term goals can be accomplished more quickly than long-term goals.

Reaching *goals* can be a powerful *boost* to your self confidence.

Getting your homework turned in on time might be a short-term goal. Long-term goals are generally accomplished over months or years. Getting a college education might be a long-term goal. Often long-term goals are made up of short-term goals.

Reaching Your Goals

To accomplish your short-term and long-term goals, you need a plan. A goal-setting plan that has a series of steps for you to take can be very effective in helping you accomplish your goals. Following a plan can help you make the best use of your time, energy, and other resources. Here are the steps of a goal-setting plan:

- Step 1: Identify a specific goal and write it down. Write down exactly what your goal is. Be sure the goal is realistic.
- Step 2: List the steps to reach your goal. Breaking big goals into smaller goals can make them easier to accomplish.
- Step 3: Get help and support from others. There are many people in your life who can help you reach your goals. They may be parents, teachers, coaches, or other trusted adults.
- Step 4: Evaluate your progress. Check periodically to see if you are actually progressing toward your goal. You may have to identify and consider how to overcome an obstacle before moving toward your goal.
- Step 5: Celebrate when you reach your goal. Give yourself a reward.

Jamie has set a goal to be chosen for the all-star team

Choosing Health Services

WHAT IS HEALTH CARE?

You will probably at some point need to seek health care services. Health care provides services that promote, maintain, or restore health to individuals or communities. The health care system is all the medical care available to a nation's people, the way they receive the care, and the way the care is paid for. It is through the health care system that people receive medical services.

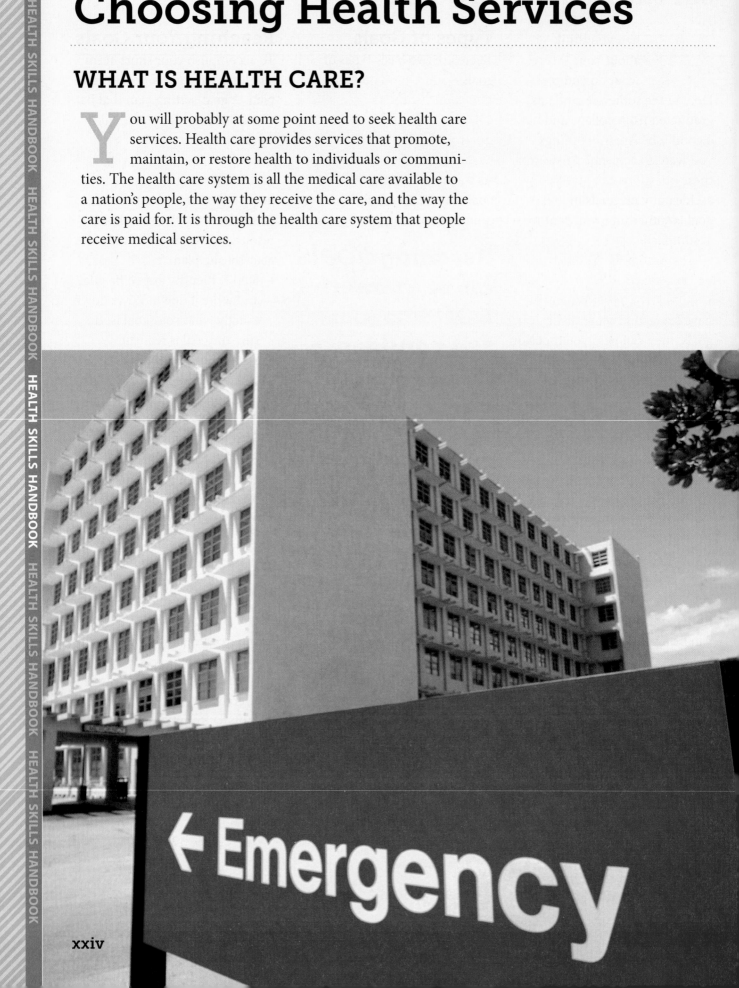

HEALTH CARE PROVIDERS

Many different professionals can help you with your health care. You may be most familiar with your own doctor who is your primary care provider: a health care professional who provides checkups and general care. Nurse practitioners and physician's assistants can also provide primary care.

In addition to doctors, nurse practitioners, and physician's assistants, many other health care professionals provide care. Nurses, pharmacists, health educators, counselors, mental health specialists, dentists, and nutritionists are all health care providers.

Preventive Care

Getting regular checkups is one way to prevent health problems and maintain wellness. During a checkup, your health care provider will check you carefully. She or he will check your heart and lungs and vision and hearing. You may also receive any immunizations you need. During your visit, your doctor may talk to you about healthful eating, exercise, avoiding alcohol, tobacco, and drugs, and other types of preventive care, or steps taken to keep disease or injury from happening or getting worse.

Specialists

Sometimes your primary care provider is not able to help you. In that case, he or she will refer you to a specialist, or health care professional trained to treat a special category of patients or specific health problems. Some specialists treat specific types of people. Other specialists treat specific conditions or body systems.

Specialist	Specialty
Allergist	Asthma, hay fever, other allergies
Cardiologist	Heart problems
Dermatologist	Skin conditions and diseases
Oncologist	Cancer
Ophthalmologist	Eye diseases
Orthodontist	Tooth and jaw irregularities
Orthopedist	Broken bones and similar problems
Otolaryngologist	Ear, nose, and throat
Pediatrician	Infants, children, and teens

Different specialists treat different conditions.

HEALTH CARE SETTINGS

Years ago, people were very limited as to where they could go for health care. In more recent years, new types of health care delivery settings have been developed. People now can go to their doctors' offices, hospitals, surgery centers, hospices, and assisted living communities.

Doctors' Offices

Doctors' offices are probably the most common setting for receiving health care. Your doctor, nurse practitioner, or physician's assistant has medical equipment to help them diagnose illnesses and to give checkups. Most of your medical needs can be met at your doctor's office.

Hospitals

If your medical needs cannot be met at your doctor's office, you may need to go to the hospital. Hospitals have much more medical equipment for diagnosing and treating illnesses. They have rooms for doing surgery and for emergency medicine. They have rooms for patients to stay overnight, if necessary. Hospitals have staff on duty around the clock every day of the year.

Surgery Centers

Your doctor may recommend that you go to a surgery center rather than a hospital. Surgery centers are facilities that offer outpatient surgical care. This means that the patients do not stay overnight. They go home the same day they have the surgery. Serious surgeries cannot be done in a surgery center. They would be done in a hospital where the patient can stay and recover. For general outpatient care, many people go to clinics.

Clinics

Clinics are similar to doctors' offices and often have primary care physicians and specialists on staff. If you go to a clinic, you might not see the same doctor each time you go. You might see whoever is on duty that day. This might make it more difficult for the doctor to get to know you and your health issues. However, for people who do not need to go to the doctor often, a clinic might be a good fit.

Hospice Care

Hospice care provides a place where terminally ill patients can live out the remainder of their lives. Terminally ill patients will not recover from their illness. Hospice workers are specially trained and are experts in pain management. They are also trained and skilled at giving emotional support to the family and the patient. Many terminally ill patients receive hospice care in their own homes. Nurses visit the patient in their own home and provide medications for pain. They also spend time with family members, helping them learn to cope during the emotionally difficult time.

Assisted Living Communities

As people get older, they may not be able to take care of themselves as well as they used to. Assisted living communities offer older people an alternative to nursing homes. In nursing homes, all of the resident's needs are taken care of. In assisted living communities, the residents can choose which services they need. They may be unable to drive and need transportation. They may need reminders to take medications. They may need to have food prepared for them. In an assisted living community, the residents are able to live in their own apartments as long as they are able. Medical staff is available when the residents need help.

PAYING FOR HEALTH CARE

Health care costs can be expensive. Many people buy health insurance to help pay for medical costs. Health insurance is a plan in which a person pays a set fee to an insurance company in return for the company's agreement to pay some or all medical expenses when needed. They pay a monthly premium, or fee, to the health insurance company for the policy. There are several different options when choosing health insurance.

Private Health Care Plans

One health insurance option is managed care. Health insurance plans emphasize preventative medicine and work to control the cost and maintain the quality of health care. Using managed care, patients save money when they visit doctors who participate in the managed care plan. There are several different managed care plans such as a health maintenance organization (HMO), a preferred provider organization (PPO), and a point-of-service (POS) plan.

Government Public Health Care Plans

The government currently offers two types of health insurance—Medicaid and Medicare. Medicaid is for people with limited income. Medicare is for people over the age of 65 and for people of any age with certain disabilities.

Following a logical plan can help you achieve many goals.

Conflict Resolution

LESSONS

1 **Conflicts in Your Life**
page 4

2 **The Nature of Conflicts**
page 8

3 **Conflict Resolution Skills**
page 12

4 **Peer Mediation**
page 15

 PREMIUM ONLINE RESOURCES

 Audio

 Videos

 Bilingual Glossary

Fitness Zone

 Web Quest

  Review

2

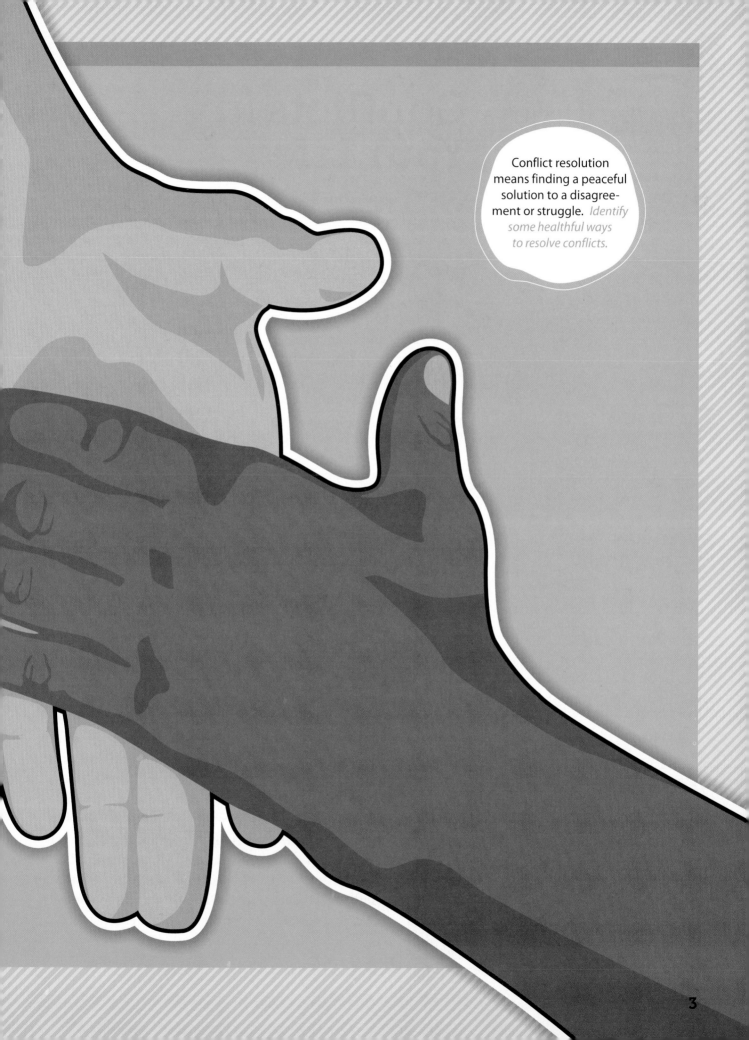

Conflict resolution means finding a peaceful solution to a disagreement or struggle. *Identify some healthful ways to resolve conflicts.*

Conflicts *in* Your Life

BIG IDEA Learning to resolve conflicts in healthful ways can help your overall well-being.

>>> **Before You Read**

QUICK WRITE List all the words that come to mind when you think of the word *conflict*.

▶ Video

>>> **As You Read**

FOLDABLES Study Organizer

Make the Foldable® on page 46 to record the information presented in Lesson 1.

>>> **Vocabulary**

> conflict
> violence
> gang
> revenge
> prejudice
> tolerance
> labeling

 Audio

🔤 Bilingual Glossary

Developing Good Character

The Myth of Positive Prejudice For example, saying that all French people are good cooks may sound like a compliment, but it is really a form of prejudice. Prejudices make assumptions based on race, culture, or group affiliations. It is unfair to assume anything about someone until you get to know that person individually.

WHAT IS CONFLICT?

MAIN IDEA Conflicts are a part of life and can be dealt with in a positive way.

Xavier and Evan both wanted to play first base in a softball game. They both became angry while insisting on playing that one position. This is an example of a conflict, or *a disagreement between people with opposing viewpoints, interests, or needs.* Conflicts happen to everyone. They are part of life.

Conflicts can involve two or more people. They can occur among strangers. Conflicts can arise between close friends or relatives. You can also experience internal conflict, or a conflict in your own mind.

Sometimes conflicts can be helpful. They can allow people to see the consequences of their behavior. When Xavier and Evan argued over who would play first base, the other players asked them to leave the game. Xavier and Evan realized their conflict hurt themselves and others.

Sometimes **conflicts** can be *helpful.*

Conflicts can be very hurtful to all parties involved. In some cases, a conflict may be only an exchange of words. Other times, conflicts can be ongoing and severe. They can damage or even destroy relationships. Conflicts can sometimes result in violence, or *an act of physical force that results in abuse.* Gang confrontations are an example of severe conflicts. A gang is *a group of young people that come together to take part in illegal activities.* Learning how to resolve conflicts in positive ways is an important health skill.

Conflicts occur for many reasons. Understanding why conflicts happen can help you prevent them. Often, conflicts occur because of an act or event. Differences of opinion or jealousy can cause conflicts.

CAUSES OF CONFLICT

MAIN IDEA Understanding what causes conflicts can help you learn to prevent them.

You will have many disagreements throughout your life. If those are settled in positive ways, you can avoid escalating conflict. Some of the issues teens argue or disagree about include:

- **Property or territory.** Sometimes teens do not respect others' property or territory. Have you ever had a disagreement with a sibling who went into your bedroom without permission?
- **Hurt feelings.** Teens may feel hurt when a friend pays attention to someone else. They may also feel hurt when they are left out of activities. Insults, teasing, and gossip can result in hurt feelings.

- **Revenge.** When someone is insulted or hurt, that person may take revenge. Revenge is *punishment, injury, or insult to a person who is seen as the cause of a strong emotion.* The other person involved may then try to get even.
- **Differing values.** Conflicts can arise when people have different values, cultures, religions, or political views.
- **Prejudice.** Sometimes conflicts are caused by prejudice, or *a negative and unjustly formed opinion.* Conflicts can arise when people are not accepted because of differences. Showing respect for all people can help avoid these types of conflicts.

A valuable tool in preventing conflicts is tolerance, or *the ability to accept other people as they are* can prevent conflict. Accepting people who are different from you can maintain positive relationships.

>>> **Reading Check**

LIST *What are five causes of conflict?*

Conflicts can arise when people have different **values, cultures, religions,** or **political views.**

COMMON CONFLICTS FOR TEENS

MAIN IDEA Conflicts can be minor or major, interpersonal, or internal.

Conflicts happen all the time. Some conflicts are minor. They may involve a simple exchange of words. Other conflicts can be major and turn violent. Gang confrontations often lead to violence. Violent conflicts that involve weapons can be dangerous or even life-threatening.

The term *conflict* usually refers to conflicts between two or more people, or interpersonal conflicts. Conflicts can also be internal. Imagine that you decide to run for class president.

Later, you learn that your best friend is also running. Campaigning against your friend may cause an internal conflict. You want to avoid competing with your friend, so you are not sure what to do.

Conflicts involving teens can occur at home or at school. For example, you and your sibling might have a disagreement over which TV show to watch at a certain time. At school, a classmate might want to copy your homework, but you know this would be against school rules.

Arguing is a common source of conflict. *Explain some skills you might use to keep an argument from getting out of control.*

Health SKILLS ACTIVITY

Decision Making

You Be the *Judge*

Mike and his friends were having a party and needed a docking station for an MP3 player. Mike borrowed his brother's docking station without asking. As Mike was riding his bike over to his friend's house, he dropped the docking station and broke it. When Mike told his brother what happened, his brother was angry. "How could you take my things without asking? I thought I could trust you," his brother said and walked away. Mike did not know what to do next. How could he mend his relationship with his brother? Analyze how Mike's behavior led to a conflict. Remember the six steps of the decision-making process.

1. State the situation.
2. List the options.
3. Weigh the possible outcomes.
4. Consider your values.
5. Make a decision and act.
6. Evaluate your decision.

With a partner, role-play a scene in which Mike thinks through his decision and then acts on it. Apply the decision-making steps. How would Mike's brother respond to his action?

Conflicts *at* Home

As you begin to grow you will find that you want more independence from your parents or guardians. This may cause conflicts at home. It is important to try to maintain a positive relationship with all family members to reduce the likelihood of conflicts occurring.

Many conflicts that arise between teens and their families occur over limits. Teens usually want fewer limits than their parents or guardians are willing to allow. For example, Juan joined some friends, but promised his parents that he would be home by 10:00 p.m. During the evening, his friends encouraged him to stay out until midnight. When Juan arrived home, his parents were angry that he broke the curfew set for him.

While teens like Juan want greater freedom, their parents want them to be safe. Parents may also require that teens contribute more to the household.

Conflicts between parents and teens are very common. Characterize how you might respond when you are told something you do not want to hear.

This can be a source of conflict. Try to remember that parents and guardians set limits and expectations to help teens grow and develop. In many families, teens can gain greater freedom by showing their parents that they are willing to take on added responsibility within the family.

Siblings can also be a source of conflict at home. Sometimes siblings do not respect one another's space or property. You might have a brother or sister who uses your property without asking for permission. Respecting each other's property and space and discussing these issues regularly can help keep conflicts to a minimum.

⟩⟩⟩ Reading Check

IDENTIFY *What is a common source of conflict among teens and their parents or guardians?*

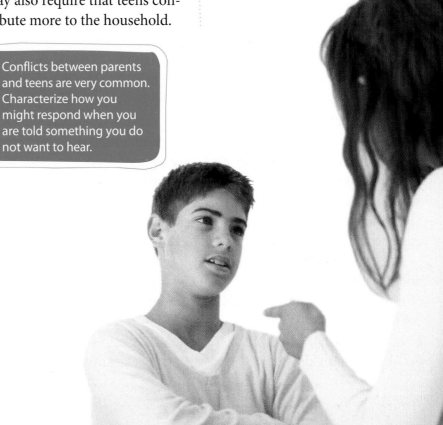

Conflicts *at* School

Many of the conflicts teens have outside of the home occur at school. Conflicts at school may involve teachers or administrators. Teens might also experience conflicts with friends, peers, or acquaintances at school.

Conflicts often arise from differences in personality, beliefs, and opinions. Conflicts can also be the result of an innocent mistake or other incident. For example, imagine you are standing in line to get into the basketball game. Someone bumps into you, causing you to bump into the person in front of you. The person ahead of you turns around and is upset with you for bumping him or her. That person may say something that upsets you, and before you know it, you are in a conflict. In this type of case, the conflict may begin with a simple exchange of words. However, it could escalate into pushing and shoving or an even more serious form of physical violence.

Bullying is *never* okay.

Conflicts may be one-sided and unprovoked. This can be caused by people not taking the time to understand one another. It can also be caused by people seeking power and attention by putting others down. This type of behavior is called bullying. Bullying is not always physical. It can come in many forms, including words or threats.

Bullying behaviors include:
- Teasing someone or saying hurtful things to a person.
- Labeling, or *name-calling,* based on prejudice.
- Leaving a person out of group activities or events.
- Sending untrue or hurtful e-mails or text messages.
- Becoming physically violent.

Bullying is never okay. No one deserves to be bullied. Use the resources available to you to make your environment as safe as possible. If you are a target of bullying, here are some ways to stop it when it happens:
- **Tell the bully to stop.** Look at the person and speak in a firm, positive voice with your head up. Explain that if the bullying continues, you will report the behavior.
- **Try humor.** This works best if joking is easy for you. Agreeing with a bully in a humorous way could catch that person off guard.
- **Walk away and stay away.** Do this if speaking up seems too difficult or unsafe.
- **Avoid physical violence.** Try to walk away and get help if you feel physically threatened. If violence does occur, protect yourself, but avoid doing anything that might escalate it.
- **Find an adult.** If the bullying is taking place at school, tell a teacher, counselor, or other school official immediately.

>>> **Reading Check**

DEFINE *What is bullying?* ∎

LESSON 1

REVIEW

>>> **After You Read**

1. **DEFINE** What is a conflict?
2. **LIST** What are three causes of conflicts among teens?
3. **IDENTIFY** What are the two main places teens have conflicts?

>>> **Thinking Critically**

4. **ANALYZE** Ivan and his dad argued about the amount of time Ivan spends playing video games on his computer. Ivan is feeling angry with his dad. What can they do to maintain a positive relationship with each other?
5. **APPLY** Imagine you have a younger sister who gets into your belongings without your permission. This makes you upset and angry. How can you resolve this issue?

>>> **Applying Health Skills**

6. **ANALYZING INFLUENCES** In what ways does the media misinform teens about how to handle conflicts? Why do you think the media portrays conflicts in these ways?

🄲 Review

🔊 Audio

The Nature *of* Conflicts

BIG IDEA Factors that make conflicts worse include anger, jealousy, group pressure, and the use of alcohol and other drugs.

>>> **Before You Read**

QUICK WRITE Write a short paragraph explaining the way you tend to resolve conflicts. How effective are the results?

▶ Video

>>> **As You Read**

STUDY ORGANIZER Make the study organizer on page 46 to record the information presented in Lesson 2.

>>> **Vocabulary**

› escalate

› mob mentality

 Audio

Bilingual Glossary

Developing Good Character

Citizenship When an argument is developing, you can show good citizenship by encouraging those involved to find a positive way to resolve the conflict. However, if the conflict turns violent, do not get involved. Instead, get help from a trusted adult right away. Identify an appropriate person at your school to whom you could report a fight.

HOW TO SPOT A CONFLICT

MAIN IDEA Conflicts can often be resolved if the signs of conflict are recognized early.

Conflicts generally occur because you and another person have different viewpoints. However, a disagreement does not need to result in conflict. Recognizing the signs of conflict early is the key to resolving them.

- **Disagreement** If you have a disagreement, be aware that this can lead to conflict.
- **Strong Emotions** Anger, sadness, jealousy and other emotions can be an early sign of conflict. Learn to control your emotions or to walk away to avoid conflict.
  - **Body Language and Behavior** Have you noticed that when some people get angry, they might ball their hands into fists or get a mean look on their face? You might cross your arms or tighten your lips. The other person might start to ignore you. These can be warning signs that a conflict is about to begin.

Managing Your Anger

Sometimes conflicts escalate, or *become more serious.* You can help prevent this by identifying the emotions that cause conflicts to escalate. Anger is a normal emotion, but it can be expressed in healthful ways. Some methods of managing anger include:

- **Step away from the situation** to get your emotions under control. This allows you time to collect your thoughts. It can help to keep you from saying things you will later regret.
- **Share your feelings** with another person, such as a parent or friend. Talking about your anger can help.
- **Engage in physical activity.** Running, biking, or other physical activity can often help to diffuse angry emotions.

Once you feel that your emotions are under control, then let the other person know how you feel. Speak calmly. Remember to use "I" messages, and discuss the problem, not the person.

Handling Feelings *of* Jealousy

Have you ever felt as if someone got better treatment than you did? If you have been in a situation like that, did you feel as if you were treated unfairly? If so, you were probably experiencing jealousy. Like anger, we all feel jealous at one time or another. Perhaps another student seems good at everything. It may appear to you that he or she tries very little to succeed. It is normal to feel jealous every now and then. A feeling of jealousy can sometimes motivate you to work harder to succeed.

Have you ever *felt* as if you were **treated** *unfairly?*

However, jealousy can also result in resentment, or an ongoing feeling of being wronged. Strong feelings of jealousy may lead a person to want to get revenge. Seeking revenge can also turn a minor problem into a major conflict. One or both parties could get hurt—physically, emotionally, or socially. Managing negative feelings such as jealousy in a positive way can help you avoid these situations.

If you have feelings of jealousy, it is important to deal with them in a healthful way. Talking to a good friend or trusted adult can help. Writing in a journal can also help you better understand some of your feelings.

>>> **Reading Check**

RECALL *How can you manage feelings of anger?*

Health SKILLS ACTIVITY

Stress Management

Letting Off *Steam*

It is not always easy to know how or when to deal with anger. Sometimes you may think it is best to say nothing, only to realize later that you are still angry. When you allow anger to build, the emotion becomes like water heating up in a kettle. Eventually, you will need to let off steam. Here are some suggestions that can help you release built-up anger or frustration:

* Close your eyes and focus on relaxing and breathing.

* Find a way to turn your negative energy into positive energy. Write in a journal or work on a hobby. Look for an opportunity to laugh.

* Do some physical activity. Go for a run, bike ride, or walk.

* Talk to a friend, parent, guardian, or another trusted adult.

 With A Group Make a list of some of the different techniques each member of your group has used to redirect negative energy. Share your list with other groups in the class.

Talking about feelings of jealousy with a trusted adult is better than seeking revenge. *Identify some situations that might cause a teen to feel jealous of someone else.*

The Warning Signs of Building Conflict

Physical Signs	Emotional Signs
A knot in the stomach	Feeling concerned
Faster heart rate	Getting defensive
A lump in the throat	Wanting to cry
Balled-up fists	Not feeling valued
Cold or sweaty palms	Wanting to lash out
A sudden surge of energy	Wanting to escape

Some warning signs that a conflict are building are physical. Other signs are emotional. *Identify some other signs of building conflict.*

Group Pressure

Have you seen a public disagreement? A crowd will often form. Sometimes people gather out of curiosity. Some people, however, may begin encouraging the conflict to escalate. This type of behavior is called a mob mentality, or *acting or behaving in a certain manner, often negative, because others are doing it.*

Have you ever noticed that during a **disagreement** in public, a *crowd* will often form?

When mob mentality occurs, some people involved in the conflict might become more aggressive than they would when a conflict occurs in private.

They might get caught up in the crowd's encouragements to do harm. Individuals might forget their own values and instead begin to do what the crowd wants. Situations such as this typically do not end well. Someone is likely to get hurt, either emotionally or physically. Avoid situations such as this. Go and get an adult to help end it.

⟩⟩ Reading Check

EXPLAIN *How can pressure from a group of peers cause a conflict to escalate?*

Conflicts *and* Substance Use

Using alcohol and other drugs can worsen a conflict. When a person uses alcohol or other drugs, it can affect their emotional state. People under the influence of alcohol and other drugs lose inhibitions and behave in ways that they normally would not. In many cases alcohol and other drugs can cause a conflict to become violent. For teens, alcohol use is illegal. Using drugs, other than for their intended purpose, is illegal for everyone.

Body language can be a sign that conflict is about to begin. *Describe how this teen is showing that she does not agree with what her parent is talking about?*

CONTROLLING CONFLICTS

MAIN IDEA You can often prevent a conflict from building by handling the problem in an appropriate way.

Conflicts are a part of life. However, conflicts can be managed by handling them in ways that help prevent them from escalating. Using the strategies below can help you better handle conflicts.

- **Understand your feelings.** Anger is one of the strongest emotions involved with conflicts. If you take time to understand why you are angry, you may better understand the conflict. Some feelings last only a few minutes. Take time to let your emotions subside before dealing with a conflict.

- **Show respect for others.** It may be difficult to show respect for people who are not kind to you. Sometimes respect can overcome unkindness. It is also important to show respect for yourself. When you avoid letting others force you into doing things you are not comfortable with, you show respect for yourself.

- **See the other person's point of view.** We all have different backgrounds and points of view. If you try to understand these differences, you may be more accepting and considerate of others. This shows that you want to resolve conflicts in a positive way and avoid escalating the conflict.

- **Keep your conflicts private.** Avoid sharing information about your conflicts. If you have a conflict, find a quiet spot to share your differences with the other person.

- **Avoid alcohol and other drugs.** People who use alcohol and drugs may behave in ways that are not normal for them. The alcohol or drugs may control their behavior.

- **Leave the scene if necessary.** At times, it is best to walk away from a conflict. This allows you and the other person to think more rationally.

>>> Reading Check

EXPLAIN *Why is it important to show respect for others?* ■

LESSON 2

REVIEW

>>> After You Read

1. **DEFINE** What does the term *mob mentality* mean?
2. **RECALL** What factors cause a conflict to escalate?
3. **LIST** Name two ways to prevent conflicts from building.

>>> Thinking Critically

4. **ANALYZE** Imagine that you have walked away from a conflict. The other person involved calls you a "chicken." What would you say?

>>> Applying Health Skills

5. **PRACTICING HEALTHFUL BEHAVIORS** Compose a list of factors that can prevent conflicts from escalating. You might list *understanding your feelings, showing respect for others,* and so on. After you have made your list, indicate which items you feel you do well. Then identify which items where you need to improve. For each item where you can use some improvement, write how you can work toward improving in this area.

⟳ Review

🔊 Audio

Conflict Resolution Skills

BIG IDEA You can deal with conflict in constructive ways.

Before You Read

QUICK WRITE List two ways of communicating that could lead to conflict. Next to each, write how the same idea could be expressed in a more positive way.

▶ Video

As You Read

STUDY ORGANIZER Make the study organizer on page 46 to record the information presented in Lesson 3.

Vocabulary

> conflict resolution
> negotiation
> collaborate
> compromise
> win-win solution

 Audio

 Bilingual Glossary

Myth vs. Fact

Myth: It is okay to yell during an argument as long as you do not call someone a name or put another person down.

Fact: Yelling sets everyone on edge. It shows that you are not in control of your emotions. Taking time to calm down can help resolve an issue peacefully.

FINDING SOLUTIONS TO CONFLICTS

MAIN IDEA Conflict resolution involves solving a disagreement in a way that satisfies everyone involved in the conflict.

Sometimes the solution to a conflict is easy to find. Other times, it might be more difficult to find a solution. In cases such as this, you might be tempted to ignore the conflict and not to deal with it. Ignoring or not resolving a conflict can be damaging to a relationship. Avoiding a conflict can often make it worse.

Not resolving a **conflict** can be **damaging** to a relationship.

Conflict resolution is *a life skill that involves solving a disagreement in a way that satisfies both sides.* Conflict resolution skills enable two parties to work together toward a positive and healthful resolution to whatever problem they may have.

Using Negotiation Skills

Negotiation is *the process of talking directly to another person in an effort to resolve a conflict.* Negotiation is a powerful skill for addressing disagreements and other conflicts. During negotiation, the two parties involved in a conflict meet and share their feelings, expectations, wants, and the reasons for their wants. The purpose of the negotiating session is to arrive at a peaceful resolution to the conflict.

The T.A.L.K. strategy is often used during negotiations. This strategy allows both parties in the conflict to collaborate, or *work together,* to arrive at a solution. You may find that you are often able to build a better relationship with the other party in a conflict when you are collaborating. The T.A.L.K. strategy, which is explained in detail on the next page, can help you remember the four main steps of the conflict resolution process.

- **T**ake a time-out. Thirty minutes is usually enough time for both sides to calm down and get their emotions under control. This will allow each side to think clearly before they talk.
- **A**llow each person to talk. If both sides are calm, each side should be able to allow the other side to talk uninterrupted. It is important that each person be able to share his or her feelings calmly without being interrupted by the other person. It is also important that the speaker not use angry words or gestures.
- **L**et each person ask questions. Each person should be allowed to ask questions of the other person. Questions should be asked and answered in a calm manner. It is important for both sides to be polite and respectful.
- **K**eep brainstorming. Continue to think of creative solutions until one that satisfies both parties is reached.

It may be difficult to keep your emotions in check during negotiations. However, it is important to do so. Avoid letting your emotions keep you from trying different solutions to your problem. Negotiations can be difficult. It is important to negotiate in private, if possible. It is also important to remember some don'ts for negotiation:
- Don't touch the other person.
- Don't point a finger at the other person.
- Don't call names.
- Don't raise your voice.

There are also some do's to remember:
- Do take a break if either party begins to get angry.
- Do stop negotiations if you are threatened by the other person.
- Do leave and tell a trusted adult if you feel threatened.

Negotiations can be helpful for solving conflicts. However, remember that some issues are not open for negotiation. If something is illegal or potentially harmful to you or others, do not negotiate. Say no or use refusal skills, and if possible, leave the scene of the conflict.

>>> **Reading Check**

IDENTIFY *What are the four steps in the T.A.L.K. strategy?*

These teens are working through a disagreement. *What is the listener doing to demonstrate that he is paying attention?*

Health SKILLS ACTIVITY

Conflict Resolution

Settling a *Disagreement*

Tanisha and Chloe have been friends since elementary school. One Saturday, they agree to meet at the movies. Chloe shows up 30 minutes late. It's the third time in a row that Chloe's been late for something that they were going to do together. Because Tanisha waited for Chloe, they missed the first part of the movie. When Chloe arrives, Tanisha shouts, "You're never on time! You ruin everything!" Remember the four steps of the T.A.L.K. strategy:

* **T**ake a time-out of at least 30 minutes.

* **A**llow each person to tell his or her side uninterrupted.

* **L**et each person ask questions.

* **K**eep brainstorming to find a good solution.

Apply the steps of conflict resolution to Tanisha and Chloe's situation. Write a dialogue that shows them resolving their conflict peacefully.

Possible Outcomes *of* Negotiation

During conflict negotiation, it may be necessary for both sides to compromise, or *give up something to reach a solution that will satisfy everyone involved.* Compromise works well when negotiating such things as which television program to watch or what to have for dinner. However, for some issues, such as whether to accept a ride from someone who has used alcohol, compromise is not a solution. Laws, your values, school rules, and limits set by your parents should not be compromised.

Compromise works well when *negotiating.*

Negotiation is an important tool in conflict resolution. *Describe one way this teen is demonstrating a principle of conflict resolution.*

Another possible outcome of negotiation is a win-win solution, or *an agreement that gives each party something they want.* Often people think that if you negotiate, someone will win and someone will lose. A win-win solution is the best possible outcome. With a win-win solution, both sides come away with something. There are no losers, so each side is satisfied with the outcome. A win-win solution can improve a relationship if both parties feel that the other allowed them to win something.

>>> **Reading Check**

CONTRAST *What is the main difference between a compromise and a win-win solution?* ■

REVIEW

>>> **After You Read**

1. **DEFINE** What is conflict resolution?
2. **EXPLAIN** Why is it important to take a time-out before beginning a negotiation?
3. **IDENTIFY** List and explain two different outcomes of negotiation.

>>> **Thinking Critically**

4. **EVALUATE** Think of a conflict you have had. Describe how you handled the situation. How might the outcome have been different if you had used the T.A.L.K. strategy to solve the problem?
5. **DETERMINE** Why is it important to brainstorm all the possible solutions to a problem?

>>> **Applying Health Skills**

6. **COMMUNICATION SKILLS** Imagine that you are involved in a conflict with a classmate. What communication skills could you use to help reach a positive resolution?

Review

Audio

Peer Mediation

BIG IDEA Mediation can provide a solution that is acceptable to both parties.

Before You Read

QUICK WRITE Have you ever had a conflict with a friend that you were able to work out? Write two to three sentences describing what you did to help resolve the conflict successfully.

▶ Video

As You Read

STUDY ORGANIZER Make the study organizer on page 46 to record the information presented in Lesson 4.

Vocabulary

› mediation
› peer mediation
› neutrality

🔊 Audio

 Bilingual Glossary

🏃 Fitness Zone

Relieving Stress I used to try to please everyone all the time. I would take what people said about me too seriously. I got into conflicts with my classmates because of the stress. All the peer mediators at school knew me by name. Finally, one suggested physical activity to help relieve my stress. I joined the swim team, and guess what? It worked! I have less stress, I'm in better shape , and I haven't been to peer mediation for months.

WHAT IS MEDIATION?

MAIN IDEA Mediation can help the parties in a conflict work together to solve the problem.

At times you are able to resolve a conflict so that both you and the other person are satisfied with the result. You achieve a win-win solution. Knowing that you worked together to arrive at a solution makes you feel good. Unfortunately, not all conflicts are easy to resolve.

Imagine that you and a classmate have teamed up to create a project for your health class. You and your partner disagree on the method you should take to complete the project. Because of the conflict, you have not made any progress on the project.

Sometimes you will not be able to resolve a conflict on your own. You may find you need help to in order to resolve a conflict. A third person who is not involved in the conflict can help people move closer to a solution.

The process of resolving conflicts by using another person or persons to help reach a solution that is acceptable to both sides is called mediation. Mediation is similar to negotiation, except that a third party is involved. That person does not resolve the conflict. A mediator helps those involved arrive at a solution.

Sometimes you will need *help* to resolve a **conflict.**

Guidance counselors, school administrators, or other trusted adults may serve as mediators. Mediators can also be students who have been trained in mediation strategies. Some schools have peer mediation programs, in which *specially trained students listen to both sides to help resolve conflicts between teens.*

⟩⟩⟩ Reading Check

EXPLAIN *Why might you ask a mediator to help resolve a conflict?*

Fancy Collection/SuperStock

The Mediation Process

Before mediation can begin, both parties must agree to allow a mediator to try to help them. The process begins in a private location. It is important that the only people present are the two parties in conflict and the mediator. If others are present, it could be distracting to the mediation process. It can also be counterproductive if other people start to take sides in the conflict.

A mediation session usually starts with the mediator asking each of the parties involved in the conflict to present his or her side of the conflict. It is important for the mediator to listen carefully. A good mediator does not allow one party to talk while the other party is sharing his or her side. The mediator may interrupt from time to time, but only to ask questions for clarification. This is to make sure that the mediator understands the situation. Asking questions is also important to make sure that the mediator understands the point of view of each of the parties involved in the conflict.

Once the mediator understands the situation, he or she will try to help the parties come up with a solution to the conflict. The mediator and the two parties involved will brainstorm possible solutions. Then they will evaluate the solutions. Some solutions may not be practical. Other possible solutions to the conflict may not be well received by both parties.

It is **important** for a *mediator* to **listen** carefully.

Then the mediator will encourage the parties to decide on a solution. The mediator does not participate in the selection process. This choice must be made by the parties involved. Both sides of the conflict must be in agreement about the solution. If both parties are not in agreement, the solution will not work.

When following these steps, a mediator can often help the parties in conflict arrive at a solution. Sometimes the parties will have to make compromises.

Often, it may take time to agree on possible solutions. The mediator may have to ask additional questions to find out what might be acceptable to the two sides. The overall solution to the conflict, however, must be acceptable to both parties.

In order to be effective, mediators must be able to both talk and listen. A mediator must be able to help parties communicate without taking sides. Mediators must also be able to help resolve any new conflicts that might arise during the mediation session. Some important traits of a successful mediator include being:
- a good communicator.
- a good listener.
- fair.
- neutral.
- an effective problem solver.

An effective mediator must always be a person who can avoid taking sides in a dispute. A mediator must also respect the privacy of the parties involved and keep all the details secret.

>>> **Reading Check**

IDENTIFY *What are two skills shared by effective mediators?*

Steps in the Mediation Process

1. The parties involved in the conflict agree to seek an independent mediator's help.

2. The mediator hears both sides of the dispute.

3. The mediator and the parties work to clarify the wants and needs of each party.

4. The parties and mediator brainstorm possible solutions.

5. The parties and mediator evaluate each possible outcome.

6. The parties choose a solution that works for each of them.

A key element to successful mediation is cooperation. Each party must be willing to work with the other and the mediator. *Explain how a mediator helps people in a conflict find a solution.*

Being *a* Peer Mediator

As mentioned before, many schools have peer mediation programs. In these programs, student mediators help other students solve their conflicts. What does it take to become a peer mediator?

Peer mediators must like to help others and be good problem solvers. They must also be able to maintain neutrality, or *a promise not to take sides,* during the mediation process. Another important trait for mediators is to be a good communicator.

During the mediation process, the peer mediator determines that both sides agree to mediation. Then the rules are explained. Generally, each party in the conflict is allowed to tell its side without being interrupted by the other party. The mediator then restates what has been said to make sure that everyone understands. The mediator then identifies what the conflict is and seeks agreement from both parties.

At this point, the mediator tries to determine what each side wants. Sometimes students want to remain friends. Knowing what each side wants, helps the mediator determine what solutions might work. After a solution is reached, the students might be asked to sign a paper that says a solution was agreed upon.

> One trait of an effective peer mediator is good listening skills. *Explain why you think it is important for a peer mediator to have these traits.*

What does it take to **become** a *peer mediator?*

Does the idea of becoming a peer mediator sound interesting to you? If so, you might want to find out whether your school has a peer mediation program. Many schools like to use peer mediators because it allows teens to put problems into words that other teens understand. If you decide to become a peer mediator, you will need to go through training. Peer mediators volunteer their services, so training would likely happen on your own time. Find out whether your school has a peer mediation program. If your school has a program and you are interested, ask how you can get involved.

>>> **Reading Check**

ASSESS *What do you think is the most important trait of a mediator?* ■

Problem Solver
Easy to Talk to
Enthusiastic
Responsible

Mature
Effective Listener
Decisive
Interested
Alert
Trustworthy
Open-minded
Reliable

LESSON 4

REVIEW

>>> **After You Read**

1. **DEFINE** What is neutrality?
2. **LIST** What are five traits of a good peer mediator?
3. **EXPLAIN** When should the parties of a conflict turn to mediation?

>>> **Thinking Critically**

4. **APPLY** Think about a conflict you have experienced. Then explain how your conflict resolutions skills helped or could have helped you reach a solution.

>>> **Applying Health Skills**

5. **CONFLICT RESOLUTION** Imagine you are involved in a conflict with a classmate. Your teacher doesn't seem to understand your problem, so you go the peer mediation program at your school. One of the other students acts as your mediator and your conflict is eventually resolved. Both you and your classmate are satisfied with the result. Why do you think you were able to work out the issue with the peer mediator and not with the teacher?

↻ Review
🔊 Audio

Hands-On HEALTH ACTIVITY

One Story, Three Endings

WHAT YOU WILL NEED

* The story: Omar and Lou are playing basketball. Peter asks if he can play.
* Ending #1: Omar says, "Sure." Lou doesn't like Peter and would rather he didn't play. However, he just shrugs and starts playing poorly. Peter asks what's bothering him. Lou says, "Nothing."
* Ending #2: Omar says, "Sure." Lou claims that Peter cheats and hogs the ball. Peter replies, "You don't want me to play because I'm better than you." Lou throws the basketball down and walks away.
* Ending #3: Omar says, "Sure." Lou says no because Peter hogs the ball. Omar suggests they trade off after every three shots so no one will have to wait long. They all agree and start to play.

WHAT YOU WILL DO

In a small group, read the story with each of the three endings. Then answer these questions for each of the three endings: Does this solution make someone angry? Do the boys try to listen to one another? Do they understand one another's feelings?

WRAPPING IT UP

You should be able to recognize the three conflict resolution styles in the three endings of the story. The best ending is when problem solving takes place.

Conflicts happen because people have different wants, needs, and opinions. There are at least three ways to handle conflict: denial, confrontation, and problem solving. Denial is when people don't admit they are angry and don't talk about their feelings. Confrontation happens when people are not willing to listen to one another or refuse to compromise. Problem solving occurs when people are able to talk about a problem without insulting or blaming one another.

foton/Tetra Images/Getty Images

READING REVIEW

FOLDABLES and Other Study Aids

Take out the Foldable that you created for Lesson 1 and any study organizers that you created for Lessons 2–4. Find a partner and quiz each other using these study aids.

LESSON 1 Conflicts in Your Life

BIG IDEA Learning to resolve conflicts in healthful ways can help your overall well-being.

* Conflicts are a part of life and can be dealt with in a positive way.
* A conflict is a disagreement between people with opposing viewpoints, interests, or needs.
* Understanding what causes conflicts can help you learn to prevent them.
* Common causes of conflict involve disputes over property or territory, hurt feelings, a desire for revenge, differing values, and prejudice.
* Conflicts can be minor or major, interpersonal, or internal.

LESSON 2 The Nature of Conflicts

BIG IDEA Factors that cause conflicts to build include anger, jealousy, group pressure, and the use of alcohol and other drugs.

* Conflicts can often be resolved if the signs of conflict are recognized early.
* Anger and jealousy are normal emotions that can be managed in healthful ways.
* You can often prevent a conflict from building by handling the problem in an appropriate way.
* Strategies for handling conflicts in healthful ways include understanding your feelings, showing respect for others, and seeing other people's points of view.

LESSON 3 Conflict Resolution Skills

BIG IDEA You can deal with conflict in constructive ways.

* Conflict resolution involves solving a disagreement in a way that satisfies everyone involved in the conflict.
* Negotiation is a powerful skill for addressing disagreements and resolving conflicts.
* The T.A.L.K. strategy allows both parties in a conflict to work together to arrive at a solution.
* Possible outcomes of negotiation include reaching a compromise or coming up with a win-win solution.
* Negotiation often requires collaboration in order to reach a positive resolution to a conflict.
* If you are faced with a potentially harmful or illegal situation, do not negotiate—instead, say no, use your refusal skills, or leave the scene.

LESSON 4 Peer Mediation

BIG IDEA Mediation can provide a solution that is acceptable to both parties.

* Mediation is a process that can help the parties in a conflict work together to solve the problem.
* Mediation requires agreement from both parties to work toward a positive solution.
* A good mediator is a good communicator, listens well, is fair and neutral, and is an effective problem solver.
* A mediator can be either a trusted adult or a student who is trained in peer mediation strategies.

 Review

 Web Quest

ASSESSMENT

Reviewing Vocabulary *and* Main Ideas

> conflict
> escalate
> mob mentality
> prejudice
> revenge
> labeling
> jealousy
> tolerance

>> On a sheet of paper, write the numbers 1–8. After each number, write the term from the list that best completes each statement.

LESSON 1 Conflicts in Your Life

1. A(n) _____ is a disagreement between people with opposing viewpoints, ideas, or goals.

2. _____ is a negative and unjustly formed opinion, usually against people of a different racial, religious, or cultural group.

3. _____ is punishment, injury, or insult to the person seen as the cause of the strong emotion.

4. Name calling based on prejudice is known as _____.

5. A valuable tool in preventing conflicts is _____, or the ability to accept other people as they are.

LESSON 2 The Nature of Conflicts

6. A conflict that becomes more serious is said to _____.

7. People who act or behave in a certain and often negative manner because others are doing it are expressing a _____.

8. _____ can lead to feelings of anger and resentment or a desire to get revenge.

>> On a sheet of paper, write the numbers 9–15. Write *True* or *False* for each statement below. If the statement is false, change the underlined word or phrase to make it true.

LESSON 3 Conflict Resolution Skills

9. The *T* in the T.A.L.K. strategy stands for <u>Tell the other person to cooperate</u>.

10. When a conflict is resolved to the satisfaction of both parties, a <u>win-lose</u> solution has been achieved.

11. <u>Negotiation</u> is the process of talking directly to another person in an effort to resolve a conflict.

12. An arrangement in which each side gives up something to reach a satisfactory solution is known as a <u>resolution</u>.

LESSON 4 Peer Mediation

13. Mediation can help two people unable to reach a compromise on their own.

14. When a mediator promises <u>to take sides</u> in a conflict, that person is maintaining neutrality.

15. Peer mediation involves having specially trained <u>teachers</u> listen to both sides in a conflict to help the parties resolve a conflict.

 eAssessment

>> Using complete sentences, answer the following questions on a sheet of paper.

Thinking Critically

16. **EVALUATE** Which step in the peer mediation process do you think would be the most challenging? Explain your answer.

Write About It

17. **EXPOSITORY WRITING** Write a story about an imaginary conflict between two people. Tell how conflict-resolution skills were used to bring about a win-win solution.

STANDARDIZED TEST PRACTICE

Reading

The following are observations made by famous people about conflict. Read the quotes, and then answer the questions.

A. "Conflict is inevitable, but combat is optional." — Max Lucado

B. "The aim of argument, or of discussion, should not be victory, but progress." — Joseph Joubert

C. "A good manager doesn't try to eliminate conflict; he tries to keep it from wasting the energies of his people. — Robert Townsend

D. "You can't shake hands with a clenched fist." — Indira Gandhi

E. "Chance fights ever on the side of the prudent." — Euripedes

1. The two quotes that suggest conflict is a fact of life are
   A. A and B.
   B. B and C.
   C. A and C.
   D. D and E.

2. Which two quotes carry the message that one should be open-minded yet cautious when experiencing a conflict?
   A. The quotes by Max Lucado and Robert Townsend
   B. The quotes by Joseph Joubert and Indira Gandhi
   C. The quotes by Robert Townsend and Indira Gandhi
   D. The quotes by Joseph Joubert and Euripedes

DEALING WITH CONFLICT

Conflicts are a normal part of life, but when you understand why they happen, you can learn ways to prevent them.

COMMON CONFLICTS FOR TEENS

AT HOME
- Limits set by parents
- Sibling disagreements
- Hurt feelings

AT SCHOOL
- Revenge or hurt feelings
- Differences or prejudice
- Bullying

CONFLICT RESOLUTION SKILLS

Use the **T.A.L.K.** strategy:

TAKE A TIME-OUT

ALLOW EACH PERSON TO TALK

LET EACH PERSON ASK QUESTIONS

KEEP BRAINSTORMING

In the **United States,**
48 states
have **anti-bullying** laws.

More than **25%**
of all **teens** in the **U.S.**
say they have been
bullied at school.

Every year, **8 out of 10**
U.S. schools report
serious crimes
involving students.

In **25** other countries,
1 in 10 students
say they have been
BULLIED at school.

PREVENTING VIOLENCE

Violence is a major health problem in the United States, sending thousands of young people to the hospital each year.

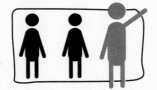

1 IN 3 students report having been in a physical **fight** in the past year.

UNDERSTANDING TEEN VIOLENCE

Most teens do not engage in violence, but teens are influenced by:

 PREJUDICE
An unfair negative opinion of a group

 MEDIA
Most teens witness 200,000 acts of violence on TV before age 18.

 PEER PRESSURE
Negative influences from others

 GANGS
Groups of people who take part in illegal activities

 DRUGS
Teens who use drugs are more likely to engage in violence.

 WEAPONS
People who carry guns are more likely to be hurt by violence.

 **TEENS ARE TWICE AS LIKELY AS ADULTS TO BE VICTIMS OF VIOLENCE.**

Protecting yourself

AVOID EVER PICKING UP A GUN, KNIFE, OR OTHER WEAPON.

MAKE SURE YOUR VALUABLES ARE HARD TO GRAB.

IF THREATENED, GIVE UP YOUR VALUABLES.

MAKE SURE YOUR FAMILY ALWAYS KNOWS WHERE YOU ARE.

OPEN THE DOOR ONLY FOR PEOPLE YOU KNOW.

AVOID GIVING PERSONAL INFORMATION.

Staying safe online

Before meeting an online friend, ask yourself:

IS YOUR ONLINE FRIEND REALLY ANOTHER TEEN?

HAVE YOU SHARED YOUR PLANS WITH YOUR FAMILY?

ARE YOU MEETING IN A SAFE, PUBLIC PLACE?

ARE YOU SURE IT'S A GOOD IDEA?

...

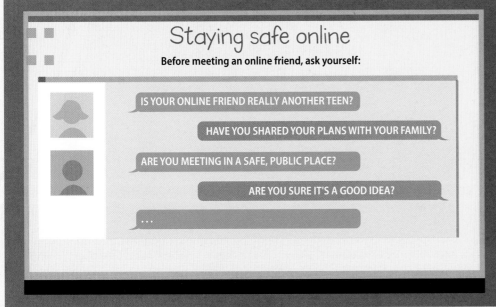

Seek help from:

- **Crisis hot lines**
- **Shelters**
- **Counseling**
- **9-1-1**

Violence Prevention

LESSONS

1 **Understanding Violence**
page 26

2 **Violence Prevention**
page 29

3 **Abuse**
page 33

4 **Preventing and Coping with Abuse**
page 38

 PREMIUM ONLINE RESOURCES

 Audio

 Videos

Bilingual Glossary

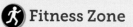 Fitness Zone

 Web Quest

 Review

Violence is an act of physical force that results in injury or abuse. *How might violence also affect the mental/emotional and social sides of your health triangle?*

Understanding Violence

BIG IDEA Violence is a major health problem in our society.

Before You Read

QUICK WRITE What steps do you take to keep yourself safe? Write a paragraph about these strategies.

▶ Video

As You Read

FOLDABLES Study Organizer

Make the Foldable® on page 47 to record the information presented in Lesson 1.

Vocabulary

- violence
- intimidation
- bullying
- harassment
- assault
- rape
- homicide
- gang
- victim

🔊 Audio

🔤 Bilingual Glossary

VIOLENCE IN SOCIETY

MAIN IDEA Many factors contribute to the violence in society.

Have you ever noticed how many news stories are about acts of violence? **Violence** is *any behavior that causes physical or psychological harm to a person or damage to property*. Popular TV shows, movies, music, and video games often feature violent content.

Violence can take many *forms*.

Violence is a major national health concern. A Centers for Disease Control and Prevention study found that violence sends more than 750,000 young people to the hospital each year.

Types *of* Violence

Violence can take many forms. Sometimes words can be violent. Name-calling and teasing can be forms of **intimidation,** or *purposely frightening another person through threatening words, looks, or body language.*

Intimidation can also be a form of **bullying,** or *the use of threats, taunts, or force to intimidate someone again and again.*

Spreading rumors can sometimes be a form of bullying. Harassment also uses words as a form of violence. **Harassment** (huh·RAS·muhnt) is *ongoing conduct that offends a person by criticizing his or her race, color, religion, disability, or gender.* Harassing words can be either written or spoken.

The most common violent crimes in the United States are assault, robbery, rape, and homicide. An **assault** is *an attack on another person in order to hurt him or her.* More assaults are reported than any other type of violent crime in the U.S. Robbery involves the taking of another's property by force. **Rape** is *forced sexual activity.* **Homicide,** which is also known as murder, is *a violent crime that results in the death of another person.* In addition to robbery, other property crimes include burglary and vandalism.

Reading Check

IDENTIFY *What are the four most common violent crimes in the U.S.?*

FACTORS IN TEEN VIOLENCE

MAIN IDEA A variety of factors influence teens toward violence.

One way to defeat violence is through education. *Cite an example of a way to help others learn to avoid homicide, rape, and assault.*

Some teens use violence to get respect from their peers. Others use it to show their independence. Some use it when they feel they are being controlled and think it is their only choice.

Most teens do not engage in violence.

Many teens who engage in violence have similar risk factors. Often, teens who use violence have seen violence at home. Teens who commit violence may not have learned to deal with feelings such as anger in healthful ways. They may engage in risk behaviors.

Playing violent video games can affect the way teens think about violence. *Explain how playing violent video games might affect a teen's thinking.*

However, most teens do not engage in violence. Teens who are aware of the risk factors may be able to avoid violent behavior. Other factors that may contribute to violence include prejudice, peer pressure, media influence, gangs, drugs, and weapons.

- **Prejudice** Prejudice is an unfair negative opinion of a group of people. Prejudice can lead to hate crimes. A hate crime is an illegal act that targets a member of a particular group of people.
- **Peer pressure** Pressure from others may cause a teen to go against his or her personal values. In some cases, a group might pressure a teen into committing a violent act.
- **Media influence** Studies show that by age 18, teens will see thousands of violent acts on TV. Violence is also a common theme in movies, music, and video games. Research shows a link between media influences and teen violence.

- **Drugs** Studies show that teens who use drugs are more likely to engage in acts of violence. Drugs and alcohol affect your judgment and your ability to make healthful decisions.
- **Gangs** Some teens join a gang to gain a sense of belonging, for protection, or because a family member or friend has joined. A **gang** is *a group of people who come together to take part in illegal activities.* Gang members may carry weapons, sell drugs, and commit acts of violence.
- **Weapons** In a recent survey, 17 percent of teens admitted to carrying a gun or other weapon at some point. Statistics show that people who carry guns are more likely to be injured as a result of gun violence.

>>> Reading Check

EXPLAIN *What is the relationship between gangs, weapons, and drugs?*

EFFECTS OF VIOLENCE

MAIN IDEA Victims of violence can suffer physical as well as mental and emotional effects.

A teen is twice as likely as an adult to be a victim of violent crime. A **victim** is *any individual who suffers injury, loss, or death due to violence.* Violent crimes always have an effect on the survivors. They may have physical injuries. They may also have emotional injuries.

At times, emotional injuries may be more difficult to handle than physical injuries. Survivors of violent crimes may need help to recover. A trusted adult or mental health professional can help. With the right help, victims of violent crime can recover.

People who experience violent crimes may be reluctant to report them. A rape victim may feel ashamed or embarrassed. That person might even feel partly to blame. A person who has been raped is never to blame for the attack.

However, if you do experience a violent crime, you can take action not only to help yourself but also to protect others.

- **Get medical attention.** You may have injuries you are not aware of. You may be in a state of shock, which can temporarily block out pain.
- **Report the incident to the police.** It is important to file a report. This will help bring the responsible person to justice and help prevent that person from harming someone else.
- **Get treatment for the emotional effects of the crime.** A violent crime is a traumatic experience. Professionals can help you work through the emotional and psychological pain caused by the crime. Counseling can help survivors of crime recover from the experience. They can then move on with their lives.

>>> **Reading Check**

IDENTIFY *What should you do if either you or a loved one were to experience a violent crime?* ■

A school counselor can be one source of help for people who experience violence. *Identify some other sources of help for survivors.*

REVIEW

>>> **After You Read**

1. **EXPLAIN** What is violence?
2. **LIST** What are six factors that contribute to violent behavior?
3. **IDENTIFY** What are three actions that the subject of a violent crime should take?

>>> **Thinking Critically**

4. **ANALYZE** Why should the survivor of a violent crime tell someone about it?
5. **APPLY** Imagine that you have just started attending a new school. Some of the other students tease you because you are new. After a couple of weeks, the teasing continues and becomes more vicious. What should you do?

>>> **Applying Health Skills**

6. **REFUSAL SKILLS** Your friend's brother has recently joined a local gang. You know that the gang sometimes commits violent crimes. They also use drugs and carry weapons. You are approached about joining the gang. How would you respond?

⟳ Review

🔊 Audio

David Burch/Getty Images

Violence Prevention

BIG IDEA You can help prevent violence.

Before You Read

QUICK WRITE Find a news article about someone who has experienced crime or violence. Write a one-paragraph summary of the story.

 Video

As You Read

STUDY ORGANIZER Make the study organizer on page 47 to record the information presented in Lesson 2.

Vocabulary

› zero tolerance policy
› youth court

🔊 Audio

🔤 Bilingual Glossary

Developing Good Character

Speaking Out About Violence Good citizenship includes helping to keep your school safe. If you know about any violence at school or violent activity that might take place, tell school officials right away. Find out whether your school has a special hotline or other way to report rumors of violent activity. If your school does not, think about how you can feel safe when reporting a potentially dangerous situation. *Write your ideas in a brief paragraph.*

PROTECTING YOURSELF FROM VIOLENCE

MAIN IDEA You can take a number of steps to help protect yourself from violence.

Acts of violence can happen anywhere, including at home, at school, or in your neighborhood. However, you can take a number of steps to help protect yourself. You can learn to avoid unsafe situations that may lead to violence.

- Remember that guns can cause serious injury or death. Avoid picking up a gun, even if you think it is unloaded.
- If a stranger stops his or her car to ask you for help or directions, walk or run in the opposite direction. Do not get close to the car.
- Avoid carrying your backpack, wallet, or purse in a way that is easy for someone to grab.
- If another person threatens you with violence, give that person the money or valuable. Your safety is more important than your possessions.

- Make sure your family always knows where you are, where you are going, and when they can expect you to be home.
- Walk with a friend. After dark, walk only in well-lit areas. Avoid dark alleyways and other places where few people are nearby.
- When you are at home, lock your doors and windows. Open the door only for people you know. If your family has a rule against answering the door, do not open it at all.
- Avoid giving out personal information when you answer the phone or respond to a text message or e-mail. Do not tell anyone you are home alone.

You can *learn* to avoid unsafe **situations** that may *lead* to **violence.**

You can also take steps to protect yourself from gangs. If you live in an area that has gang activity, avoid wearing gang-related colors or clothing. When you are walking on the streets, avoid wearing expensive jewelry. Avoid carrying expensive electronics that might be a target of theft. Another way to help stay safe from gang violence is to choose friends who are not members of a gang.

Practicing safe habits online is another way to protect yourself.

If you are like many teens, you may communicate with many people online. However, avoid meeting an online friend without first learning more about that person.

- Is your online friend really another teen? Sometimes, an adult who could harm you may pretend to be a teen online.
- If you do agree to meet an online friend in person, share your plans with a parent or another trusted adult.

- Make sure you meet your online friend in a public place. First-time meetings are always safer in an area where other people are around in case you need help.

During the teen years, many people form new friendships and start to date. Remember that healthy friendships are built on respect, caring, and honesty. If a friend or dating partner becomes violent or abusive, avoid that person and tell a parent or other trusted adult.

WAYS TO REDUCE VIOLENCE

MAIN IDEA Everyone can make an effort to help reduce the spread of violence.

Violence affects victims, their families, and the rest of society. According to the U.S. government, violence costs the country more than $158 million a year. This figure includes property damage as well as law enforcement and health care costs.

What can you do to *reduce* or *stop* violent behavior?

Acts of violence can damage property, cause injury, and even ruin lives. However, each individual can do his or her part to help reduce violent activity. This often means taking action to stop violence before it starts. What can you do personally to help reduce violent activity?

- Develop your own personal zero tolerance policy regarding violence. A zero tolerance policy *makes no exceptions for anyone for any reason.* This might include making a commitment never to fight with, bully, or threaten others.
- Encourage others to resolve conflicts peacefully. By doing this, you can be a role model for nonviolence. You can set a positive example for others.
- Encourage your family to become a member of a Neighborhood Watch program. These programs include volunteers who work closely with law enforcement.
- Report any acts of violence you witness. Talk to your parents, guardians, or a trusted adult and ask what you should do. The adult may help you contact law enforcement.

In addition to the steps listed, you can also become an advocate, or supporter, of safety and victims' rights. One organization you could become involved with is Youth Outreach for Victim Assistance (YOVA). This program is sponsored by the National Center for Victims of Crime. It is a youth-adult partnership that educates teens about what victims experience. This group tells young people where they can go for help if they experience violent crime. You can also search online or contact local law enforcement to learn about other ways you can have a positive impact.

>>> **Reading Check**

EXPLAIN *Why should you tell a trusted adult when you witness an act of violence?*

Many schools today are stepping up measures to prevent acts of violence. *What steps have officials in your school taken to make you feel safer?*

Reducing Violence *in* Schools

You spend a lot of time at school, so it is important to know what your school does to help keep you safe. Most schools are safe places. Each year, however, more than 3 million students report having experienced some type of crime at school. Two million of these crimes are violent. Many schools have taken steps to reduce violence on campus.

It is *important* to **know** what your **school does** to *help keep you safe.*

- **Zero tolerance policies.** Many schools have adopted zero tolerance policies. In schools that have such a policy, any student who brings a weapon to school is expelled. Students who participate in violent acts are also expelled.

- **School uniforms.** Some schools use dress codes or uniforms to help keep students safe. When all students wear similar clothing, it is not easy to tell whether one student is wealthy and another is not. As a result, there may be less violence. Dress codes and uniforms also affect gang members. Dress codes make it difficult for gang members to dress in clothing that shows what gang they are in.

- **Security systems.** Many schools have security systems. They may limit entry to just one door. All of the other doors are kept locked. They may have metal detectors, security cameras, or security guards. These help keep weapons out of schools. Schools may also have a school resource officer from the local police department. Resource officers are usually on campus during school hours. They get to know the students, which helps to prevent problems.

- **Locker searches.** Some schools periodically search students' lockers. Schools may also search students' backpacks. Sometimes trained dogs are brought in by the police. The dogs are used to sniff out drugs and weapons.

- **Conflict resolution programs.** More and more schools are educating students in conflict resolution. A youth court is *a special school program where teens decide resolutions for other teens for bullying and other problem behaviors.* Peer mediation is also popular. These programs involve teens working to help other teens resolve problems in nonviolent ways.

In addition to these efforts, remember some of the actions you can take to help stop violence at school. Become a role model for nonviolence by encouraging others to resolve their differences peacefully. Report any acts or rumors of violence you see or hear about.

NEIGHBORHOOD CRIME WATCH

We immediately report all SUSPICIOUS PERSONS and activities to our Police Dept.

Many communities work together with law enforcement to make their neighborhoods safer. *What is being done in your community?*

Reducing Violence *in* Communities

Students can often influence their peers to make healthful choices. In some schools, students have started their own programs to help reduce violence and criminal activity. They put their ideas into practice in their school and in their community.

Communities are also taking steps to reduce violence. Some communities use their resources to create after-school programs. These programs may be academic, recreational, or cultural. They offer a safe place for teens to spend their afternoons. Teens can stay until their parents or guardians get home from work.

Improved lighting in parks and at playgrounds is another way communities work to reduce violence. Crimes are less likely to happen in well-lighted areas. People who commit crimes are more likely to be seen and recognized if the area has plenty of good lighting.

Protect yourself by avoiding **dangerous** situations.

Neighborhood Watch programs are also popular in many communities. Members of the program watch their neighborhoods for signs of trouble. They report to authorities if they see suspicious activities.

Some communities put their patrol officers on foot, on bicycles, or on horses. This allows the officers to be closer to the people they serve. Police get to know people in the community. This helps law enforcement to prevent criminal activity.

You can protect yourself by avoiding dangerous situations. Walk directly to and from your home. Travel with another person or in a group, especially at night. Avoid taking shortcuts through unfamiliar or unsafe areas of your community.

>>> **Reading Check**

LIST *What are four ways schools are working to reduce violence?* ■

LESSON 2

REVIEW

>>> **After You Read**

1. **EXPLAIN** What are communities doing to prevent the spread of violence?
2. **RECALL** What can you do to help reduce the spread of violence?
3. **IDENTIFY** What are schools doing to help eliminate violent behavior at school?

>>> **Thinking Critically**

4. **ANALYZE** Some people claim that school searches violate a person's privacy. How would you respond to this claim?
5. **APPLY** What strategies could you use to keep yourself safe walking home from a mall?

>>> **Applying Health Skills**

6. **GOAL SETTING** Choose one way you can help to reduce the spread of violence at school or in your community. Use the goal-setting steps you have learned to make an action plan to help reduce violence. Show your plan to your teacher. Follow your action plan for a week, and then write a paragraph discussing your experience.

 Review

 Audio

S. Meltzer/PhotoLink/Getty Images

Abuse

BIG IDEA Abuse affects the physical, mental/emotional, and social health of the person who is abused.

Before You Read

QUICK WRITE Write a paragraph that describes problems that might affect a relationship. Identify healthy ways of dealing with the problems.

▶ Video

As You Read

STUDY ORGANIZER Make the study organizer on page 47 to record the information presented in Lesson 3.

Vocabulary

› abuse
› battery
› domestic violence
› neglect
› sexual abuse

 Audio

 Bilingual Glossary

Myth vs. Fact

Myth: Child abuse does not run in families. Fact: People who abuse children were often abused themselves during childhood. However, not everyone who was abused as a child will become an abuser later in life. Survivors of abuse can make the choice not to continue the pattern. It is often necessary to seek help to learn new strategies for responding when angry.

WHAT IS ABUSE?

MAIN IDEA Abuse can happen in various ways and take many forms.

Relationships, even close ones, have their good days and bad days. In a healthy relationship, people respect and care for each other. Relationships can be unhealthy, though. Sometimes relationships become unbalanced and difficulties arise. When this happens, abuse can occur. **Abuse** is *the physical, mental, or emotional mistreatment of another person.*

Abuse is never the fault of the person who is being abused. It can affect people of all ages, races, and economic groups. All forms of abuse are wrong and harmful. A person who is being abused should report it to the authorities. Teachers, counselors, nurses, and physicians are required to report suspected abuse to the police. Police investigate reports of abuse to determine whether or not a crime has been committed.

Types *of* Abuse

The four main types of abuse are physical abuse, emotional abuse, neglect, and sexual abuse. You will learn more about these types of abuse as you read the rest of this lesson. In the next lesson, you will also learn strategies for preventing and coping with abuse. Remember, though, that abusive relationships and situations should never be tolerated.

> *Abuse* is never the **fault** of the person who is being *abused.*

Abuse can occur in all kinds of situations. Many times, abuse takes place within a family or other close relationship. For instance, a child may be abused by a parent or guardian. One spouse may be abused by the other spouse. A sibling may abuse a brother or sister. A family member may abuse an older relative. Again, however, abuse is never acceptable behavior.

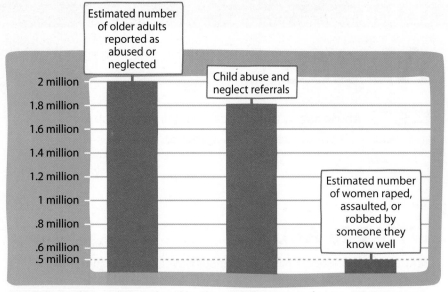

Estimated number of older adults reported as abused or neglected

Child abuse and neglect referrals

Estimated number of women raped, assaulted, or robbed by someone they know well

2 million
1.8 million
1.6 million
1.4 million
1.2 million
1 million
.8 million
.6 million
.5 million

Sources: National Research Council on Elder Abuse, U.S. Department of Justice, U.S. Department of Health and Human Services.

Abuse can happen to people of all ages. *Why do you think people in certain age groups may be more likely to be abused?*

Abuse can also occur between dating partners. Healthy dating relationships are based on each partner respecting the other. When one partner doesn't respect the other, abuse may occur. The abuse may be physical, emotional, or psychological.

Often, abusers will try to make the people they abuse believe that they deserve to be treated harshly. This is never true. Abuse is not the same as discipline. A parent may use discipline, such as a time-out or grounding, to correct behavior or help shape a person's character. On the other hand, abuse causes severe harm to a person—physically, mentally/ emotionally, or socially. No one ever deserves to be abused.

⟫⟫ Reading Check

IDENTIFY *Name some ways in which a person can be affected by abuse.*

Abuse is **not** the same as *discipline.*

Physical Abuse

Physical abuse causes physical harm. A common form of physical abuse is battery, or *the beating, hitting, or kicking of another person.* This is never acceptable behavior. Battery is common in cases of domestic violence, or *physical abuse that occurs within a family.* This situation is where most abuse happens. Domestic violence is about power and control. In such cases, the abuser tries to keep strict control over one or more family members. When physical abuse results from domestic violence, it is considered to be assault. Assault is a crime and should be reported to the police.

Domestic violence includes pushing, slapping, punching, and choking another family member. Sometimes household items are used as weapons. In many cases of domestic violence, physical abuse does not happen all the time. The abuser may engage in other unacceptable behavior in between incidents of assault or battery.

Children who are abused may not get the medical attention they need. Often, when a young victim of abuse is taken for medical attention, the abuser makes excuses for the injuries. For instance, the abuser might claim that the child is clumsy and fell down or ran into something. The abuser might also claim that the young person gets hurt often because he or she is accident prone. Similar excuses are often used when the person who has been abused is an older adult.

Emotional Abuse

Physical abuse often leaves physical signs. It may not be as obvious that a person is being emotionally abused. However, the effects of emotional abuse can be harmful too. The effects of emotional abuse may last even longer than the effects of physical abuse.

The effects of _emotional abuse_ may last even longer.

Emotional abuse involves words and gestures. These are used to make a person feel worthless, stupid, or helpless. Bullying, yelling, and teasing are all forms of emotional abuse. Insults, harsh criticism, and threats of violence are also forms of emotional abuse. People who have been emotionally abused often feel bad about themselves.

Emotional abuse can occur in the home, at school, or with friends. Sometimes emotional abuse occurs in a dating situation. For example, your partner may be very jealous and want to know where you are all of the time. Your partner may keep you from spending time with family and friends. These are forms of emotional abuse. If you or someone you know has been emotionally abused, get help from a trusted adult.

Neglect

Every person has needs. We all need food, clothing, and shelter. We also need medical care and education. Children need supervision and someone else to provide for them. Sometimes parents or guardians do not meet these needs. **Neglect** is _the failure to provide for the basic physical and emotional needs of a dependent._ This type of abuse sometimes also affects older family members who cannot care for themselves.

People also have emotional needs. People need to feel loved and nurtured. If caregivers do not provide for the needs of the people who depend on them, they may be guilty of neglect. Neglect is against the law and should be reported to the police.

About one out of every ten children in the U.S. is a victim of neglect or child abuse. That means that each year about ten percent of the children are not having their needs met. Neglect can have long-lasting effects on children. Physical injuries can harm a child's growth and development. A neglected child may also have mental/emotional and social problems throughout life.

>>> **Reading Check**

INFER _Why are children more likely to be targets of neglect?_

Emotional abuse can make a person feel isolated or unwanted. _Describe ways you could you reach out to a person who needs help._

Sexual Abuse

Every two minutes, someone in the United States is sexually abused. Sexual abuse is *sexual contact that is forced on another person.* This can be any type of unwanted touching, kissing, or sexual activity. Photographing a child for sexual materials is another form of sexual abuse. It is also against the law to force a child to look at sexual materials. Sexual abusers often target younger people. A child may be abused by someone who is known and trusted. The abuser may be a family member or a family friend or acquaintance.

Sexual abuse is a type of violence, but abusers may act in other ways toward their victims.

They may try to trick or bribe a child to perform sexual acts. Sexual abuse is never okay. It is damaging to the person who has been sexually abused. Sexual abuse is always a crime. It needs to be reported to the police.

Sexual harassment is another form of sexual abuse. Sexual harassment may happen at school. It includes words, touching, jokes, looks, notes, or gestures with a sexual manner or meaning. Sexual harassment is illegal and should be reported to school personnel immediately.

It can be difficult for a person who has been abused to talk about it. *If you thought someone was being abused, who might you suggest that person turn to?*

Health SKILLS ACTIVITY

Communication Skills

Using "I" Messages

Sometimes a person who makes ethnic jokes or inappropriate remarks may be a friend of yours. He or she may not realize that you find this conduct offensive or abusive. When a friend behaves in a way that offends you, you need to let him or her know that you are offended by these actions. At the same time, you may not want to jeopardize the friendship or create a conflict. You can express your feelings in a positive way by using "I" statements instead of "you" statements. Here are a few examples of "you" statements that can be substituted with "I" statements.

Instead of "You" Statements...	...Use "I" Statements
You're being offensive...	...I am offended by what you are saying.
You're embarrassing me.	...I feel embarrassed.
You aren't being funny.	...I don't think that is funny.

With A Group

You and the other members of your group should each write three "you" statements. Exchange papers and change the "you" statements to "I" statements.

EFFECTS OF ABUSE

MAIN IDEA People who experience abuse can experience long-term effects.

Physical scars from abuse may go away after time. That is not always the case with the emotional scars. People who experience abuse may blame themselves. They may be afraid or ashamed to get help. Children who suffer abuse or neglect often have a number of problems.

If *you* or someone you *know* experiences **abuse,** seek *help.*

Physical health concerns as a result of abuse include:

- Impaired brain development.
- Impaired physical, mental, and emotional development.
- A hyper-arousal response by certain areas of the brain. This may result in hyperactivity and sleep disturbances.
- Poor physical health, including various illnesses.

Mental/emotional health consequences of abuse include:

- Low self-esteem.
- Increased risk for emotional problems such as depression, panic disorder, and post-traumatic stress disorder.

- Alcohol and drug abuse.
- Difficulty with language development and academic achievement.
- Eating disorders.
- Suicide.

Abuse may also result in various social health consequences:

- Difficulty forming secure relationships.
- Difficulties during adolescence.
- Criminal and/or violent behavior.
- Abusive behavior.

It is important for people who have been abused to deal with their feelings. Help is available from many resources. If you or someone you know experiences abuse, seek help or encourage him or her to get help. Talk to a parent or guardian, a teacher, school counselor, or other trusted adult, or the police. ∎

Abuse can affect the physical, social, and mental/emotional health of a person who has been abused. *Name some specific effects of abuse.*

LESSON 3

REVIEW

>>> **After You Read**

1. **DEFINE** What is abuse?
2. **DESCRIBE** Name and describe the four major types of abuse.
3. **IDENTIFY** What are four social health concerns for survivors of abuse?

>>> **Thinking Critically**

4. **ANALYZE** Why are children and older adults often the subjects of abuse?
5. **EVALUATE** Do you think it is important for survivors of abuse to get help? Why or why not?

>>> **Applying Health Skills**

6. **ADVOCACY** Locate and research local agencies and organizations that provide help for people who have experienced abuse. For each agency or organization, write down the name, contact information, and whether they specialize in a particular type of abuse. Make copies of the list for your school counselor to give to students.

Ⓖ Review

🔊 Audio

Preventing *and* Coping with Abuse

BIG IDEA The cycle of abuse can be stopped, but it often requires outside help.

Before You Read

QUICK WRITE Think about adults you trust. Then write one or two sentences that describe what makes those adults trustworthy.

▶ Video

As You Read

STUDY ORGANIZER Make the study organizer on page 47 to record the information presented in Lesson 4.

Vocabulary

› cycle of abuse
› crisis hot line

 Audio

Ⓐ Bilingual Glossary

Developing Good Character

Helping a Victim of Abuse If someone you know has been a target of violence, you can show concern and compassion for that person. You can listen if the person wants to talk. You can help him or her know when to seek help from a parent or other trusted adult. Identify some communication skills that would be helpful in this type of situation. Describe some other ways in which you could show the person that you care.

WARNING SIGNS OF ABUSE

MAIN IDEA Abuse has warning signs and risk factors.

You may notice injuries, such as bruises and burns, on a person who has been abused. The person may have no explanation for the injuries. Sometimes a person who is being abused might appear to be withdrawn or depressed. A person who is being abused may also become aggressive toward others. If you can spot the signs of abuse, you may be able to help.

All families have problems now and then. Usually the problems are dealt with in healthful ways. Good communication skills can help families solve problems in healthful ways. However, some families may not know how to handle problems when they arise. This can lead to extra stress. The stress of family problems can also increase the risk of abusive behavior.

If you can learn to *spot* the **signs** of **abuse,** you may be able to *help.*

The Cycle *of* Abuse

Often, abuse in a family may have begun long ago. Health experts have found that patterns of abuse may go back many generations. A generation is a group of people who are born at about the same time. For example, you, your parents, and your grandparents make up three generations. Although it is not always the case, a child who has been abused or who witnessed abuse may grow into an adult who abuses others. This cycle of abuse, or *pattern of repeating abuse from one generation to the next,* does not have to continue forever in a family. However, breaking the cycle of abuse often requires outside help.

Reading Check

DEFINE *What is a cycle of abuse?*

HELP FOR SURVIVORS OF ABUSE

MAIN IDEA Many resources are available to help people who have been abused.

Abuse in a family affects the whole family. It affects the abuser, the person who has been abused, and other relatives who may not live in the same household. The effects can be long-lasting. Even if a child only witnesses abuse, he or she may grow up thinking abuse is acceptable behavior. In such cases, every member of the family needs help. They need to learn that abuse is not acceptable.

Why Survivors Stay Silent

Many people who have been abused do not tell anyone about it. This prevents them from getting the help they need. Survivors of abuse might choose not to report it for many reasons. Some of the reasons people who have been abused stay silent include:

- Some adults who have been abused think that no one else will believe them.
- A child may fear that adults will think that he or she is lying or exaggerating.
- A person may think that abuse is a private matter.
- Some people may believe that they deserved the abuse because of something they did wrong. However, no one ever deserves to be abused.
- A person may think their abuser will seek revenge.

Men and boys often think that because they are males, they should be able to protect themselves from abuse. This is not true. Abusers usually have an advantage over their victims. They may be stronger or older.

Warning Signs of Abuse

- Illness
- Divorce
- Lack of communication and coping skills
- History of having been abused as a child
- Alcohol or other drug use
- Unemployment and poverty
- Feelings of worthlessness
- Emotional immaturity
- Lack of parenting skills
- Inability to deal with anger

This table presents some factors that can increase the risk of a person becoming abusive. *Explain how identifying and working to improve these factors can help prevent abuse.*

An abuser may be in a position of trust and authority. Abusers may try to make a person feel afraid. A threat can be powerful enough to prevent a victim from reporting the abuse. They may threaten to harm the victim and that person's family if the victim tells.

People who experience abuse should **seek help** for *themselves* and for their *abusers.*

Sometimes, adults who experience domestic violence make excuses for their injuries or for their abuser. This behavior is called enabling. Enabling creates an atmosphere in which a person can continue unacceptable behavior. It can also allow the abuser to avoid taking responsibility for his or her actions. Enabling can establish a cycle or pattern of abuse. If an abuser feels as if he or she will not face consequences for the abuse, it is likely to continue. Sometimes enabling is a result of fear experienced by people who are abused. People who experience abuse should instead seek help for themselves and for their abusers. As you will learn in this lesson, many resources are available to help someone who is being abused. Remember, a person who is abused is never to blame for the abuse.

⟫⟫ Reading Check

IDENTIFY *What are three reasons that people who are abused often stay silent?*

Sources of Help for Victims of Abuse

If you have a friend you think is being abused, try talking to that person about it. Encourage your friend to seek help. If your friend is too afraid to seek help, go talk to a trusted adult yourself. Let the adult know that you are concerned and worried that your friend is being abused. Remember that child abuse is a crime, and it should be reported to the police.

Talking with a parent or other trusted adult can be one way to help make abuse stop. A crisis hot line, or a *toll-free telephone service where abuse victims can get help and information,* is another resource. Crisis hot lines offer many types of assistance to people who have been abused.

Services provided by crisis hot lines may include help for the abused person, family members, and others who may be affected. People who answer the phones at hot lines have been trained to deal with abuse problems. They know how to help people who have been abused. The caller's identity is kept anonymous.

These organizations help people who have been abused by providing hot lines where people can talk about abuse and get advice. *Identify some others who may be helped by these organizations.*

Crisis hot line conversations are always kept confidential. The figure at the bottom of this page lists information about hot lines that provide help for people who have been abused. Additional hot line numbers can be found online or in the phone book.

If your *friend* is being **abused,** encourage the *friend* to **seek help.**

Breaking the Cycle of Abuse

Each person has the power to help end the cycle of abuse. People who have been abused—especially children—often feel ashamed. This is especially true if the abuse was sexual. People who have experienced domestic violence may have similar feelings. A person might be afraid that the family will be separated if news of the abuse gets out. A child might also be afraid of getting the abuser in trouble.

However, the cycle of abuse will not end until it is reported. Again, a person who is abused needs help, and so does the abuser. If the abuse is reported to police, the abuser may go to court. As a result, the abuser may be required to seek treatment. If the abuser can learn to manage his or her behavior in more healthful ways, it can help end the cycle of abuse.

Abusers will often threaten their victims or make them promise not to tell anyone. Abuse can also create fear, which can result in enabling. As you have learned, enabling can allow an abuser to continue his or her unacceptable behavior. If you or someone you know is being abused, remember that keeping it secret is not healthful. The only way anyone will get help is if the abuse is reported. Remember that many people have experienced abuse. People who have been abused have many sources of help.

>>> **Reading Check**

RECALL *What types of services do crisis hot lines provide?*

Organization	Whom They Help
Childhelp USA	Child abuse victims, parents, concerned individuals
Youth Crisis Hotline	Individuals reporting child abuse, youth ages 12 to 18
Stop It Now!	Child sexual abuse victims, parents, offenders, concerned individuals
National Domestic Violence Hotline	Children, parents, friends, offenders
Girls and Boys Town	Abused, abandoned, and neglected girls and boys, parents, and family members

NAIC, U.S. Department of Health and Human Services.

Recovering *from* Abuse

Many times, people who have been abused need help in order to recover. Professional counselors are trained to help people overcome emotional trauma. A counselor can help a survivor of abuse by helping the person understand his or her feelings. The person may feel fear or shame. A counselor can also help a survivor learn ways to manage these kinds of emotions. Group counseling is another option. In these sessions, people can meet and talk with others who have also experienced abuse.

Recovery is possible for both the **victim** and the **abuser.**

It is also possible to leave an abusive situation. Children and families who have ongoing problems with abuse may escape to shelters. Shelters are community-run residences where people can feel safe. Families can stay together in shelters, away from the abuser. They can stay while they get help putting their lives back together.

If you have experienced abuse, use what you have learned to get help. If you suspect a friend has been abused, share your knowledge. Encourage that person to get help. Remember that with help, recovery is possible for both the victim and the abuser.

⟩⟩⟩ Reading Check

IDENTIFY *What are some sources of help for people who have been abused?* ■

Help is available in any community for people who have been abused and their families. *List some resources that students in your school can turn to if they need to report an abuse problem.*

REVIEW

⟩⟩⟩ After You Read

1. **IDENTIFY** What are three warning signs of abuse?
2. **EXPLAIN** What is the cycle of abuse?
3. **LIST** Why do some people not report abuse?

⟩⟩⟩ Thinking Critically

4. **ANALYZE** Why are some abusers older than their victims?
5. **EVALUATE** Why do you think crisis hot lines keep their callers' identities anonymous?

⟩⟩⟩ Applying Health Skills

6. **COMMUNICATION SKILLS** Write a dialogue between yourself and a person who has been abused. That person wants to report the problem, but doesn't know where to begin.

Ⓒ Review

⏺ Audio

ZenShui/Alix Minde/Getty Images

Hands-On HEALTH ACTIVITY

Learning to *Manage* Threats *by* Working Together

WHAT YOU WILL NEED

* Poster board
* Markers or crayons

WHAT YOU WILL DO

1 Your teacher will assign each of four small groups one of the following threatening behaviors: harassment, intimidation, emotional abuse, and bullying.

2 In your group, brainstorm nonviolent ways of responding to the threatening situation. First, imagine an instance in which the threatening behavior takes place. Discuss how a young person might respond in a positive way.

3 Create a colorful poster. On one side, describe the situation your group was assigned. On the other side, write "A Nonviolent Response." Below that, write a nonviolent way of responding.

WRAPPING IT UP

After all the groups have presented their posters, discuss ways teens can help other teens respond to threatening situations in positive ways. Display your posters to help your classmates and other students learn a variety of nonviolent responses.

When faced with a threatening situation, a common reaction is to lash out in anger. When people are pushed, either physically or emotionally, they want to push back. This chapter presents a number of different situations that are threatening, which include harassment, intimidation, emotional abuse, and bullying. When you are faced with a threatening situation, be prepared to respond in a nonviolent way. This activity can help you learn some nonviolent responses.

Blend Images/Getty Images

READING REVIEW

FOLDABLES and Other Study Aids

Take out the Foldable® that you created for Lesson 1 and any study organizers that you created for Lessons 2–4. Find a partner and quiz each other using these study aids.

LESSON 1 Understanding Violence

BIG IDEA Violence is a major health problem in our society.

* Many factors contribute to the violence in society.
* The most common violent crimes in the U.S. are assault, robbery, rape, and homicide.
* Name-calling, teasing, and making threats are types of violence that can be forms of intimidation.
* A variety of factors influence teens toward violence.
* Victims of violence can suffer physical as well as mental and emotional effects.

LESSON 2 Violence Prevention

BIG IDEA You can help prevent violence.

* You can take a number of steps to help protect yourself from violence, including avoiding unsafe situations.
* Everyone can make an effort to help reduce the spread of violence.
* You can help stop violence by encouraging others to resolve conflicts peacefully and by reporting violent activity.
* Schools and communities have taken action to help stop acts of violence and criminal behavior.

LESSON 3 Abuse

BIG IDEA Abuse affects the physical, mental/emotional, and social health of the person who is abused.

* Abuse can happen in various ways and take many forms.
* The four main types of abuse are physical abuse, emotional abuse, neglect, and sexual abuse.
* People who experience abuse can experience long-term effects.
* If you or someone you know has experienced abuse, seek help or encourage that person to get help.

LESSON 4 Preventing and Coping with Abuse

BIG IDEA The cycle of abuse can be stopped, but it often requires outside help.

* Warning signs of abuse include physical injuries and emotional symptoms.
* Major risk factors for abuse include various types of stress within a family or relationship.
* Each person has the power to do his or her part to help end the cycle of abuse.
* Many resources are available to help people who have been abused.

 Review

 Web Quest

ASSESSMENT

Reviewing Vocabulary and Main Ideas

> assault
> homicide

> youth court
> victim

> violence

> zero tolerance
policy

>> On a sheet of paper, write the numbers 1–6. After each number, write the term from the list that best completes each statement.

LESSON 1 **Understanding Violence**

1. _____ is any behavior that causes physical or psychological harm to a person or damage to property.

2. The killing of one human being by another is known as _____.

3. A(n) _____ is any individual who suffers injury, loss, or death due to violence.

4. An unlawful threat or attempt to do bodily injury to another person is known as _____.

LESSON 2 **Violence Prevention**

5. A _____ is a policy that makes no exceptions for anybody for any reason.

6. A _____ is a special school program where teens decide resolutions for other teens for bullying and other problem behaviors.

>> On a sheet of paper, write the numbers 7–12. Write *True* or *False* for each statement below. If the statement is false, change the underlined word or phrase to make it true.

LESSON 3 **Abuse**

7. A common type of abuse is <u>zero tolerance</u>.

8. Children, <u>older adults</u>, and people with disabilities all may be targets of neglect.

9. <u>Physical abuse</u> involves words and gestures used to make a person feel worthless, stupid, or helpless.

LESSON 4 **Preventing and Coping with Abuse**

10. The <u>cycle of abuse</u> is a pattern in which children of abuse go on to become abusers.

11. If abuse is ongoing or violent, family members may go to community-run residences known as <u>crisis hot lines</u>.

12. <u>Enabling</u> creates an atmosphere in which a person can continue unacceptable behavior and can establish a pattern of abuse.

✔ eAssessment

>> Using complete sentences, answer the following questions on a sheet of paper.

Thinking Critically

13. **ANALYZE** A teen named Tom lives in a community that has gangs. He often sees gang members in his neighborhood on his way to and from school. Tom does not want to become a victim of gang violence. What are some ways Tom could help keep himself safe?

14. **APPLY** You have learned that a friend is being abused, but your friend is afraid to seek help. What advice might you give your friend? What could you do to help stop the abuse?

Write About It

15. **EXPOSITORY WRITING** Write a paragraph describing how the media might influence violent behavior.

16. **OPINION** Use various resources to learn what your community is doing to prevent violence. Think of some additional steps that might help make your community safer. Write a blog post or letter to the editor of your local newspaper offering your suggestions on what more could be done to prevent violence where you live.

Ⓐ Ⓑ Ⓒ Ⓓ STANDARDIZED TEST PRACTICE

Math
The table below contains data about victims of violence for a 10-year period.
Use the data to answer the questions that follow.

Violent Victimization Rates by Age, 2000–2010*

Year	12 to 14	15 to 17	18 to 20
2000	5.37	5.19	5.49
2001	5.4	5.24	4.77
2002	4.68	4.82	5.24
2003	5.23	5.79	5.3
2004	4.23	4.42	4.83
2005	5.04	5.5	5.39
2006	5.08	5.12	5.6
2007	5.18	5.03	4.95
2008	5.21	4.66	3.92
2009	4.42	4.38	3.89
2010	3.32	3.37	3.76

* Victimization rates are per 1,000 persons age 12 or older.

1. The two years in which 15- to 17-year-olds experienced a higher rate of crime than 12- to 14-year-olds and 18- to 20-year-olds was
   A. 2000 and 2002.
   B. 2009 and 2010.
   C. 2003 and 2005.
   D. 2001 and 2008.

2. For the years 2008 to 2010, the mean victim rate for 18- to 20-year-olds was
   A. 3.74.
   B. 3.95.
   C. 4.04.
   D. 3.86.
   E. A and C.
   F. D and E.

CHAPTER 1

Foldables®

Make this Foldable® to help you organize what you learn in Lesson 1 about conflicts in your life.

1 Begin with a plain sheet of 11" x 17" paper. Fold the paper into thirds along the long axis, and then fold in half again lengthwise. This forms six rows.

2 Open the paper and refold the sheet into thirds along the short axis. This forms three columns.

3 Unfold and draw lines along the folds. List causes of conflict in the left column. Use the top column to list two places where conflict may occur.

As you read the lesson, fill in the chart with examples of behaviors that might cause conflicts in the places you have listed.

Study Organizers

Use the following study organizers to record the information presented in Lessons 2–4.

Lesson 2:
Key Word Cluster

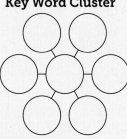

Lesson 3:
Two-Column Chart

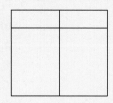

Lesson 4:
Flow Chart

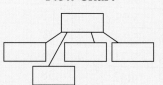

CHAPTER 2

Foldables®

Make this Foldable® to help you organize what you learn in Lesson 1 about understanding violence.

1 Begin with a plain sheet of 11" x 17" paper. Holding the paper lengthwise, fold down a 2-inch flap at the top of the sheet.

3 Unfold and write at the top of each of the three sections, *Types of Violence, Factors in Teen Violence,* and *Effects of Violence.*

2 Next, fold the paper into thirds.

As you read the lesson, fill in the chart under each of the three headings you have created with information you learn about each concept.

Study Organizers

Use the following study organizers to record the information presented in Lessons 2–4.

Lesson 2:
Index Cards

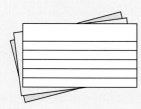

Lesson 3:
Two-Column Chart

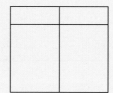

Lesson 4:
Outline

Glossary/Glosario

English

Español

A

Abstinence (AB stuh nuhns) The conscious, active choice not to participate in high-risk behaviors.

abstinencia Opción activa y conciente de no participar en comportamientos de alto riesgo.

Abuse (uh BYOOS) The physical, emotional, or mental mistreatment of another person.

abuso Maltrato físico, emocional o mental de otra persona.

Advocacy Taking action in support of a cause.

promoción Actuar en apoyo de una causa.

Assault An attack on another person in order to hurt him or her.

asalto Ataque hacia otra persona con la intención de herirla.

Attitude (AT ih tood) Feelings and beliefs.

actitud Sentimientos y creencias.

B

Battery The beating, hitting, or kicking of another person.

asalto Dar palizas, golpear o dar puntapiés a otra persona.

Bullying A type of violence in which one person uses threats, taunts, or violence to intimidate another again and again.

intimidar Tipo de violencia en la cual una persona usa amenazas, burlas, o actos violentos para intimidar a otra persona una y otra vez.

C

Collaborate Work together.

colaborar Trabajar juntos.

Communication The exchange of information through the use of words or actions.

comunicación Intercambio de información a través del uso de palabras y acciones.

Compromise When both sides in a conflict agree to give up something to reach a solution that will satisfy everyone.

compromiso Cuando los dos lados de un conflicto concuerdan con dejar algo de lado para alcanzar una solución que satisfaga a todos.

Conflict A disagreement between people with opposing viewpoints, interests, or needs.

conflicto Desacuerdo entre dos personas con puntos de vista, intereses o necesidades opuestas.

Conflict resolution A life skill that involves solving a disagreement in a way that satisfies both sides.

resolución de un conflicto Habilidad que implica el hecho de resolver un desacuerdo satisfaciendo a los dos lados.

Crisis hot line A toll-free telephone service where abuse victims can get help and information.

linea de reporte de crisis Servicio telefónico sin pago en cual víctimas de abusos pueden recibir ayuda e información.

Cultural background The beliefs, customs, and traditions of a specific group of people.

base cultural Creencias, costumbres y tradiciones de un grupo específico de personas.

Culture the collected beliefs, customs, and behaviors of a group

cultura Colección de creencias, costumbres y comportamientos de un grupo.

Cumulative (KYOO myuh luh tiv) risk When one risk factor adds to another to increase danger.

riesgo acumulativo Cuando un factor riesgoso se suma a otro e incrementa el peligro.

Cycle of abuse Pattern of repeating abuse from one generation to the next.

ciclo de abuso Patrón de repetición del abuso de una generación a la siguiente.

English

Español

D

Decision making The process of making a choice or solving a problem.

tomar decisiones Proceso de hacer una selección o de resolver un problema.

Domestic violence Physical abuse that occurs within a family.

violencia doméstica Abuso físico que ocurre dentro de una familia.

E

Environment (en VY ruhn muhnt) All the living and nonliving things around you.

medio Todas las cosas vivas y no vivas que te rodean.

Escalate To become more serious.

intensificar Llegar a ser más grave.

G

Gang A group of young people that comes together to take part in illegal activities.

pandilla Grupo de jóvenes que se juntan para participar en actividades ilegales.

Goal setting The process of working toward something you want to accomplish.

establecer metas Proceso de esforzarte para lograr algo que quieres.

H

Harassment (huh RAS muhnt) Ongoing conduct that offends another person by criticizing his or her race, color, religion, physical disability, or gender.

acoso Conducta frecuente que ofende a otra persona con críticas sobre su raza, color, religión, incapacidad física, o sexo.

Health The combination of physical, mental/emotional, and social well-being.

salud Combinación de bienestar físico, mental/emocional y social.

Health care system All the medical care available to a nation's people, the way they receive the care, and the way the care is paid for.

sistema de cuidado de la salud Servicios médicos disponibles para a la gente de una nación y las formas en las cuales estos son pagados.

Health insurance A plan in which a person pays a set fee to an insurance company in return for the company's agreement to pay some or all medical expenses when needed.

seguro médico Plan en el que una persona paga una cantidad fija a una compañía de seguros que acuerda cubrir parte o la totalidad de los gastos médicos.

Health skills skills that help you become and stay healthy

habilidades de salud Habilidades que ayudan a ser y mantenerte saludable.

Heredity (huh RED I tee) The passing of traits from parents to their biological children.

herencia Transferencia de características de los padres biológicos a sus hijos.

Homicide A violent crime that results in the death of another person.

homicidio Crimen violento que resulta en la muerte de otra persona.

Glossary/Glosario

English	Español

I

Intimidation Purposely frightening another person through threatening words, looks, or body language.

intimidación Asustar a otra persona a propósito con palabras amenazantes, miradas o lenguaje corporal.

L

Labeling Name-calling.

marcar Dar nombre.

Lifestyle factors Behaviors and habits that help determine a person's level of health.

factores del estilo de vida Conductas y hábitos que ayudan a determinar el nivel de salud de una persona.

Long-term goal A goal that you plan to reach over an extended period of time.

meta a largo plazo Objetivo que planeas alcanzar en un largo periodo de tiempo.

M

Managed care A health insurance plan that saves money by encouraging patients and providers to select lest costly forms of care.

cuidado controlado Plan de seguro médico que ahorra dinero al limitar la selección de doctores de las personas.

Media Various methods for communicating information.

medios de difusión Diversos métodos de comunicar información.

Mediation Resolving conflicts by using another person or persons to help reach a solution that is acceptable to both sides.

mediación Resolución de conflictos por medio de otra persona que ayuda a llegar a una solución aceptable para ambas partes.

Mind-body connection How your emotions affect your physical and overall health and how your overall health affects your emotions.

conexión de la mente con el cuerpo Forma en la cual tus emociones afectan tu salud física y general, y como tu salud general afecta tus emociones.

Mob mentality Acting or behaving in a certain and often negative manner because others are doing it.

mentalidad de movimiento Actuar o comportarse de cierta manera, normalmente maneras negativas, sólo porque otros lo están haciendo.

N

Neglect Failure to provide for the basic physical and emotional needs of a dependent.

abandono Fallas en el proceso de proveer las necesidades físicas y emocionales de una persona considerada como dependiente.

Negotiation (neh GOH shee AY shuhn) The process of talking directly to the other person to resolve a conflict.

negociación Proceso de hablar directamente con otra persona para solucionar un conflicto.

Neutrality A promise not to take sides.

neutralidad Promesa de no tomar partido durante un conflicto entre otros.

P

Peer mediation (mee dee AY shuhn) a process in which a specially trained student listens to both sides of an argument to help the people reach a solution

mediación de compañeros Proceso en el cual un estudiante especialmente capacitado escucha los dos lados de un argumento para ayudar a las personas a llegar a un acuerdo.

Peers People close to you in age who are a lot like you.

compañeros Personas de tu grupo de edad que se parecen a ti de muchas maneras.

Prejudice (PREH juh dis) A negative and unjustly formed opinion.

prejuicio Opinión formada negativa e injustamente.

Prevention Taking steps to avoid something.

prevención Tomar pasos para evitar algo.

Preventive care Steps taken to keep disease or injury from happening or getting worse.

cuidado preventivo Medidas que se toman para evitar que ocurran enfermedades o daños o que empeoren.

Primary care provider Health care professional who provides checkups and general care.

profesional médico principal Profesional de la salud que proporciona exámenes médicos y cuidado general.

English

Español

R

Rape Forced sexual intercourse.

Refusal skills Strategies that help you say no effectively.

Reliable Trustworthy and dependable.

Revenge Punishment, injury, or insult to the person seen as the cause of the strong emotion.

Risk The chance that something harmful may happen to your health and wellness.

Risk behavior An action or behavior that might cause injury or harm to you or others.

violación Relaciones sexuales forzadas.

habilidades de rechazo Estrategias que ayudan a decir no efectivamente.

confiable Confiable y seguro.

venganza Castigo, daño, o insulto hacia una persona por causa de una emoción fuerte.

riesgo Posibilidad de que algo dañino pueda ocurrir en tu salud y bienestar.

conducta arriesgada Acto o conducta que puede causarte daño o perjudicarte a ti o a otros.

S

Sexual abuse Sexual contact that is forced upon another person.

Short-term goal A goal that you can achieve in a short length of time.

Specialist (SPEH shuh list) Health care professional trained to treat a special category of patients or specific health problems.

Stress The body's response to real or imagined dangers or other life events.

abuso sexual Contacto sexual forzado por una persona.

meta a corto plazo Meta que uno puede alcanzar dentro de un breve periodo de tiempo.

especialista Profesional del cuidado de la salud que está capacitado para tratar una categoría especial de pacientes o un problema de salud específico.

estrés Reacción del cuerpo hacia peligros reales o imaginarios u otros eventos en la vida.

T

Tolerance (TAHL er ence) The ability to accept other people as they are.

tolerancia Habilidad de aceptar a otras personas de la forma que son.

V

Values The beliefs that guide the way a person lives.

Victim Any individual who suffers injury, loss, or death due to violence.

Violence An act of physical force resulting in injury or abuse.

valores Creencias que guían la forma en la cual vive una persona.

víctima Cualquier individuo que sufre algún daño, pérdida o muerte debido a la violencia.

violencia Acto de fuerza física que resulta en un daño o abuso.

W

Wellness A state of well-being or balanced health over a long period of time.

Win-win solution An agreement that gives each party something they want.

bienestar Mantener una salud balanceada por un largo período de tiempo.

solución de ganancia doble Acuerdo o resultado que da algo de lo que quieren a cada lado.

Y

Youth court A special school program where teens decide punishments for other teens for bullying and other problem behaviors.

corte juvenil Programa escolar especial en el cual adolescentes deciden el castigo para otros adolescentes por intimidar y otros problemas de comportamiento.

Z

Zero tolerance policy A policy that makes no exceptions for anybody for any reason.

normativa de tolerancia Normativa en que no hay excepciones para nadie por ninguna razón.

Index

Index

Index

FLIP 4 FITNESS

Flip for Fitness is for everyone. Non-athletes who avoid joining organized sports can develop a personal fitness plan to stay in shape. Even athletes can use some of the tips to cross train for their favorite sport.

Planning a Routine

Flip for Fitness helps you plan a fitness routine that helps your body slowly adjust to activity. Over time, you will increase both the length of time you spend and the number of times that you are physically active each week. Teens should aim to get at least one hour of physical activity each day. These periods of physical activity can be divided into shorter segments, such as three 20 minute segments each day. Exercise includes any physical activity, such as completing a fitness plan, playing individual or group sports, or even helping clean at home. The key is to keep your body moving.

Before You Start Exercising

Every activity session should begin with a warm-up to prepare your body for exercise. Warm-ups raise your body temperature and get your muscles ready for physical activity. Easy warm-up activities include walking, marching, and jogging, as well as basic calisthenics or stretches. As you increase the time you spend doing a fitness activity, you should increase the time you spend warming up. Check the Sample Physical Fitness Plan in Teen Health in Connect Ed.

Fitness Information *and* Resources

Fitness Apps *and* Other Resources

» 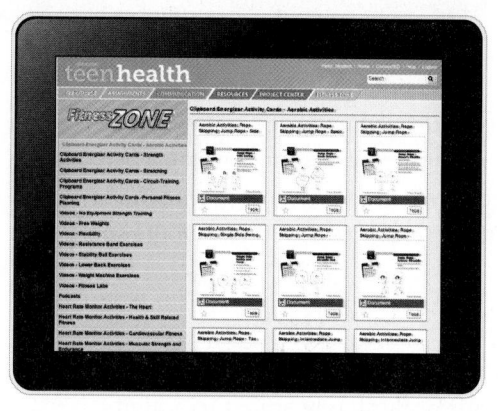 **USDA's MyPlate** The MyPlate Super Tracker is a free online fitness and diet tracker. To review the tracker, go online to https://www.choosemyplate.gov and search for "Super Tracker".

» Additionally, organizations such as the **American Heart Association** and **KidsHealth** provide resources on developing walking programs. The online addresses are: http://startwalkingnow.org and http://kidshealth.org.

» Finally, smartphone and tablet users can download several nutrition and fitness tracking apps. Many are free of charge. Use the terms "fitness", "exercise", or "workout" when searching for apps.

Accessing Information

» The *Teen Health* online program includes resources to develop your own fitness plan. Check out the **Fitness Zone** resources in ConnectEd.

» The Centers for Disease Control and Prevention's, **Body & Mind (BAM)** web site also provide fitness information. The online address is: http://www.bam.gov. Search for "physical activity" or "activity cards."

Safety Tips

On the following pages, you'll find fitness activities for groups or individuals. Each activity includes information on what you'll need, how to start, and how to stay safe. Safety is the most important factor.

⚠ Always be aware of where you are and don't take any unnecessary chances.

⚠ Obey the rules of the road while riding your bicycle, avoid unsafe areas, and use the proper safety equipment when working out.

⚠ Finally, remember to drink water and to rest between exercise sessions.

5 Elements *of* Fitness

When developing a fitness plan, it's helpful to have a goal. Maybe your goal is to comfortably ride your bike to school each day or maybe you want to complete the Tour de France in the future. Regardless of the reasons why you develop a fitness plan, focusing on the five elements of fitness will help you achieve overall physical fitness. The five elements are:

1 Cardiovascular Endurance
The ability of the heart and lungs to function efficiently over time without getting tired. Familiar examples are jogging, walking, bike riding, and swimming.

2 Muscle Endurance
The ability of a muscle or a group of muscles to work non-stop without getting tired. Many activities that build cardiovascular endurance also build muscular endurance, such as jogging, walking, and bike riding.

3 Muscle Strength
The ability of the muscle to produce force during an activity. Activities that can help build muscle strength include push-ups, pull-ups, lifting weights, and running stairs.

4 Flexibility
The ability to move a body part freely, without pain. Improve your flexibility by stretching gently before and after exercise.

5 Body Composition
The amount of body fat a person has compared with the amount of lean mass, which is bone, muscle, and fluid. A healthy body is made up of more lean mass and less body fat. Body composition is a result of diet, exercise, and heredity.

Fitness Circuit

Are you looking for a quick workout that will develop endurance, strength, and flexibility? A Fitness Circuit may be just what you need. Many public parks have Fitness Circuits (sometimes called Par Courses) with exercise stations located throughout a park. You walk or run between stations as part of your workout. A fitness circuit can also be created in your backyard or even a basement.

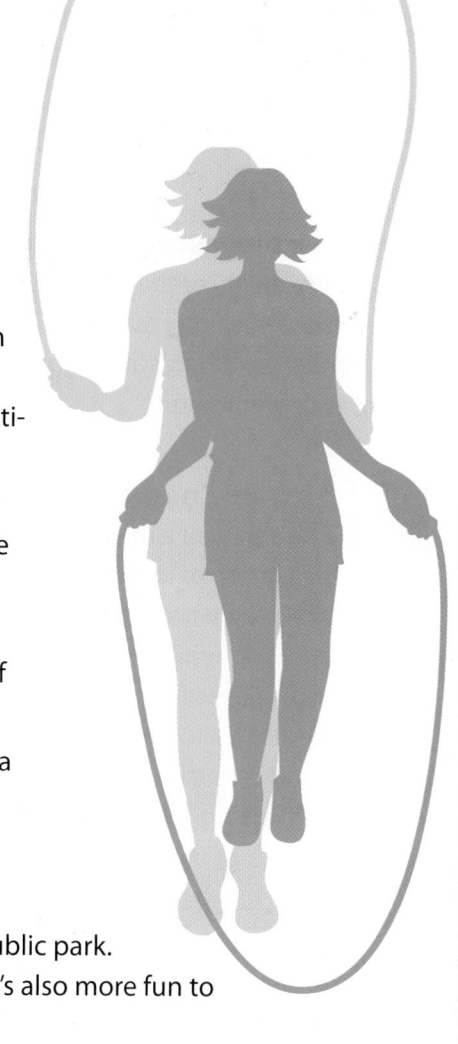

What Will I Need?

» Access to a public park or a home-made Fitness Circuit course.

» Comfortable workout clothes that wick away perspiration.

» Athletic shoes.

» Stopwatch (optional).

» Jump rope, dumbbells, exercise bands, or check out the Fitness Zone Clipboard Energizer Activity Cards, Circuit Training for ideas.

How Do I Start?

» In the park, read the instructions at each exercise station and perform the exercises as shown. Use the correct form. Try to do as many repetitions as you can for 30 seconds.

» After you finish the exercise, walk or run to the next station and complete that exercise.

» Check your heart rate to see how intensely you exercised at the end of the Fitness Circuit.

» Every month or so, consider adding a new exercise.

How Can I Stay Safe?

» Be alert to your surroundings in a public park. It is best to have a friend with you. It's also more fun to exercise with a friend.

» At home, leave enough room between stations to allow you to move and exercise freely. Avoid clutter in your exercise area.

» Perform the exercises correctly and at your own pace.

Walking

Walking is more than just a way to get from one place to another. It's also a great physical activity. By walking for as little as 30 minutes each day you can reduce your risk of heart disease, manage your weight, and even reduce stress. Walking requires very little equipment and you can do it almost anywhere. More good news: Walking is also something you can do by yourself or with friends and family.

What Will I Need?

» Running or walking shoes. Many athletic shoe stores sell both.

» Loose comfortable clothes that wick away perspiration. Layering is also a good idea. Consider adding a hat, sunglasses, and sunscreen if needed.

» Stopwatch and water bottle unless there are water fountains on your route.

» A pedometer or GPS to track your distance.

How Do I Start?

» Five minutes of easy stretching.

» Walk upright with good posture. Do not exaggerate your stride or swing your arms across your body.

» Build your time and distance slowly. One mile or 20 minutes every other day may be enough for the first couple weeks. Eventually you will want to walk at least 30-60 minutes five days a week.

How Can I Stay Safe?

» Let your parents know where you will be walking and how long you will be gone.

» Avoid wearing headphones if by yourself or if walking on a road or street.

Running *or* Jogging

Running or jogging is one of the best all-around fitness activities. Running uses the large muscles of the legs thereby burning lots of calories and also gives your heart and lungs a good workout in a shorter amount of time. Running also helps get you into condition to play team sports like basketball, football, or soccer. More good news is that running can be done on your schedule although it's also fun to run with a friend or two.

What Will I Need?

» A good pair of running shoes. Ask your Physical Education teacher or an employee at a specialist running shop to help you choose the right pair.

» Socks made of cotton or another type of material that wicks away perspiration.

» Bright colored or reflective clothing and shoes.

» A stopwatch or watch with a second sweep to time your runs or track your distance.

» Optional equipment might include a jacket or other layer depending on the weather, sunscreen, and sunglasses.

How Do I Start?

Your ultimate goal is to run at least 20 to 30 minutes at least 3 days a week. Use the training schedule shown below. Start by walking and gradually increasing the amount of time you run during each exercise session. Starting slowly will help your muscles and tendons adjust to the increased work load. Try spacing the three runs over an entire week so that you have one day in-between runs to recover.

How Can I Stay Safe?

» Use the correct equipment for the sport you have chosen.

» Running on a track, treadmill, or in a park with level ground will help you avoid foot or ankle injuries.

» Avoid running on the road, especially at night.

» Avoid wearing headphones unless you are on a track, treadmill, or another safe place. Safety experts agree that headphones can distract you from being alert to your surroundings.

Here is a plan to get you started as a runner:

» Start each run with a brisk 3-5 minute walk to warm-up.

» Take some time to slowly stretch the muscles and areas of the body involved in running. Avoid "bouncing" when stretching or trying to force a muscle or tendon to stretch when you start to feel tightness.

» Begin slowly and gradually increase your distance and speed. A good plan for the first several weeks is to alternate walking with easy running. The running plan included in this section can give you some tips on how to train for a 5K run.

» Use the "talk test." Can you talk in complete sentences during your training runs? If not, you are running too fast.

Training Schedule

M W F	Split Schedule	Duration
Week 1	Brisk 5 min. walk Walk: 60 - 90 seconds Run: 60 seconds	Repeat for 20 min.
Week 2 and 3	Brisk 5 min. walk Walk: 60 seconds Run: 60 - 90 seconds	Repeat for 20 min.
Week 4	Brisk 5 min. walk Walk: 60 seconds Run: 3 - 5 minutes	Repeat for 20 min.
Week 5+	Brisk 5 min. walk Run: 20 to 30 minutes	

Preparing *for* Sports *and* Other Activities

Do you want to play a sport? If so, think about developing a fitness plan for that sport. Some of the questions to ask yourself are: Does the sport require anaerobic activity, like running and jumping hurdles? Does the sport require aerobic fitness, like cross-country running? Other sports, such as football and track require muscular strength. Sports like basketball require special skills like dribbling, passing, and shot making. A workout plan for that sport will help you get into shape before organized practice and competition begins.

What Will I Need?

Each sport has different equipment requirements. Talk to a coach or physical education teacher about how to get ready for your sport. You can also conduct online research to learn what type of equipment you will need, such as:

» Proper footwear and workout clothes for a specific sport.

» What facilities are available for training and practice, such as a running track, tennis court, football or soccer field, or other safe open area.

» Where you can access weights and others form of resistance training as part of your training.

How Do I Start?

Now that your research is done, you can create your fitness plan. Include the type of exercises you will do each training day.

» Include a warm-up in your plan.

» List the duration of time that you will work out.

» Plan to exercise 3–5 days a week doing at least one kind of exercise each day. Remember to include stretching before every workout.

How Can I Stay Safe?

» Get instruction on how to use free weights and machines

» Make sure you start every activity with a warm-up.

» Ease into your fitness plan gradually so you do not pull a muscle or do too much too soon.

» Practice good nutrition and drink plenty of water to stay hydrated.

Interval Training

Getting fit takes time. One method, interval training, can show improvement in two weeks or less. Interval training consists of a mix of activities. First you do a few minutes of intense exercise. Next, you do easier, less-intense activity that enables your body to recover. Interval training can improve your cardiovascular endurance. It also helps develop speed and quickness.

Intervals are typically done as part of a running program. Not everyone wants to be a runner though. Intervals can also be done riding a bicycle or while swimming. On a bicycle, alternate fast pedaling with easier riding. In a pool, swim two fast laps followed by slower, easier laps.

What Will I Need?

» A running track or other flat area with marked distances like a football or soccer field.

» If at a park, 5–8 cones or flags to mark off distances of 30 to 100 yards.

» A training partner to help you push yourself (optional).

How Do I Start?

» After warming up, alternate brisk walking (or easy jogging). On a football field or track, walk 30 yards, jog 30 yards, and then run at a fast pace for 30 yards. Rest for one minute and repeat this circuit several times. If at a park, use cones or flags to mark off similar distances.

» Accelerate gradually into the faster strides so you stay loose and feel in control of the pace.

» If possible, alternate running up stadium steps instead of fast running on a track. This will help your coordination as well as your speed. Running uphill in a park would have similar benefits.

How Can I Stay Safe?

» Interval training works the heart and lungs. For this reason, a workout using interval training should be done only once or twice a week with a day off between workouts.

» Check with your doctor first. If you have any medical condition like high blood pressure or asthma, ask your doctor if interval training is safe for you.